Handbook
on the
Holy Spirit

HANDBOOK ON THE HOLY SPIRIT

Clear and Heartwarming Guidance
on His Work in the Believer's Life

Robert J. Kuglin

Christian Publications
3825 Hartzdale Drive, Camp Hill, PA 17011

Faithful, biblical publishing since 1883

ISBN: 0-87509-676-X
©1983, 1996 by Robert J. Kuglin
All rights reserved
Printed in the United States of America

96 97 98 99 00 5 4 3 2 1

Contents

Foreword

"Why is it, in a time when so many North Americans profess to be Christians, the church is having such little impact on crime and sin?" This question so many people ask points to the desperate need for revival in the church.

Bob Kuglin gives us the heartcry of a true revivalist in *Handbook on the Holy Spirit*. In practical and illustrated insights he describes the work and ministry of the Holy Spirit. He traces revival in the believer, in the church and the community.

Setting forth the need to be filled with the Holy Spirit, he shows the promise and evidence of such indwelling. He warns against "equating hyper-emotion with the moving of the Holy Spirit," so prevalent in our day.

Bob Kuglin's personal ministry prepares him as a highly qualified author of this handbook. He was called out of the pastoral ministry during the great Canadian revival which touched his own Ontario congregation in 1971 and 1972. He then became a leader in a continent-wide revival ministry.

I first came in contact with Bob Kuglin's ministry just prior to his leaving the pastorate, when he came to Florida where I was serving as the district superintendent for The Christian and Missionary Alliance. In a very quiet, unassuming way, he was anointed of God, and instrumental in bringing revival to churches in Florida and later in Georgia. Since those days his ministry has been blessed of God throughout the United States, Canada and overseas.

I believe *Handbook on the Holy Spirit* will be a blessing to those who look for a heart-warming, clear answer on the work of the Holy Spirit in the believer's life. They can experience what Dr. A.B. Simpson called, "living in heaven today."

—Dr. Paul L. Alford
President, Toccoa Falls College

Preface

This book was not really created in the mind of the author. It was born in the hearts of thousands of God's people who have sat patiently through lectures and sermons during my twenty years of ministry as a pastor and another twenty-four years as an itinerant evangelist.

For a number of years many have urged me to put my lectures on the Holy Spirit into print. I hesitated to do so—it seemed to me that the bookstores were already crowded with books on the subject. But when it was suggested that I should not only put the lectures into print, but I should also put the answers I gave to questions into the book as well, it seemed appropriate to do so.

The book may not seem to flow properly in some places. This is intentional. Over the years I discovered that the same questions were raised at the same places during the lectures. These questions did not particularly fit the study at that point. But they were the questions that repeatedly came to people's minds at that time. Therefore I have answered them at the same point in the book.

I owe much to my wife, Gwen, who at my request criticized me constructively through the years, so I could better present God's Word. She has also assisted me during the final drafting of the manuscripts with her editing and suggestions. She has been most patient when at times I left the writing to take up the ministry of evangelism, my first love.

I have not quoted authors to reinforce my teaching. In writing chiefly to laypersons, I thought it best to use my terminology rather than someone else's words. Many times when an author is quoted, another quote is needed to explain what he is saying. However, the bibliography, indicating just a few of the books that I have read, no doubt has played a large role in developing my thinking through the years.

As you commence this book on the Holy Spirit, I can think of no better way to do it than by praying the prayer of the hymn writer:

Holy Spirit, while we bend,
　　Graciously on us descend;
Like a gentle dove appear
　　To each waiting spirit here.

Holy Spirit, come within,
　　Crucify this heart of sin,
Let it die upon the cross
　　With its soul defiling dross.

Holy Spirit, life provide
　　For the heart thus crucified,

Let it break the bonds of death
   By the power of Thy breath.

Holy Spirit, I would be
   Filled, yea, wholly filled with Thee;
Come with overflowing love,
   Let me Thy sweet presence prove.

Holy Spirit, Heav'n on earth,
   Seal me with celestial birth;
Bear me on Thy wings of love
   To my blissful home above.

—G.W. Crofts

Chapter 1

Ouch! That Hurts!

A cross the top of the chalkboard I wrote, "Who or what is the Holy Spirit?" This would be my opening question to a group of mature adults in a large Canadian evangelical church.

It was vacation time and I was enjoying the usual ministerial rest—preach twice on Sunday, and teach the adult Bible class. This particular time, I had been requested to give a four-lesson series on the Holy Spirit.

What would a young pastor teach to a group of Christians, many of whom had enjoyed a Christian heritage much longer than he had? My first question would be the key that would unlock the door to the type of material that I would use. I knew the theology. But what did the people really need? Where should I start? What should be the content? And how should I conclude the series?

The question had been on the chalkboard from the time the first-comers arrived. Everyone in the class had seen the question for at least fifteen minutes as the opening "exercises" droned on and on. The chairman kept asking for more favorite songs or choruses. Or special Bible verses. Or testimonies that anyone was just waiting to give. Finally, with the response somewhat less than explosive, he said to the small group, "Come on. We have another five minutes to waste before Mr. Kuglin brings us the lesson." And waste it he did.

But perhaps God knew that I needed a little extra time to prepare myself for some of the responses to my totally simple question. Originally, I had intended that the question should read only, "Who is the Holy Spirit?" But thinking that might generate a very limited response, I finally settled for the longer question which would give the adults greater leeway with their answers.

I began the lesson by reading aloud what each class member must have read a number of times as they sat waiting for class to begin: "Who or what is the Holy Spirit?"

"The Third Person of the Trinity," responded a lady who had graduated from a recognized Bible college in 1931.

"The Paraclete," observed her husband.

"The Comforter," declared another.

"Anything else?" I kept asking when the answers were in the right vein.

"Our guide," declared another.

"A teacher," suggested one who was obviously a schoolmarm of many years' standing.

I kept writing these in order on the chalkboard. To some answers I responded, "We will come back to that later," but wrote them across the board the same as the rest.

"A divine influence," offered another gentleman.

"The wind," stated one very emphatically. "The pastor preached about it not so long ago."

This opened up a whole series of water, oil, fire, breeze, gold, seal, fan, people and other things, some right and some wrong. Then, though I should not have asked it again, I did: "Anything else?"

"It is a Who," came the startling response.

That answer came from a man who accepted Christ when he was a child. He was also four years my senior. Where did he get such an answer? Where had he been all these years of good Bible teaching?

I knew every pastor he had had—all of them men of God. Two of them became Bible college presidents, and another became a district superintendent. There was not a poor Bible teacher among them all. He had been taught in Sunday school and from the pulpit that the Holy Spirit is a Person.

But he never grasped this truth. Or he had refused to believe it. To him the Holy Spirit was merely an influence, a *thing*. So putting together what he had been taught with what he really believed he came up with, "It is a Who."

It was then that I realized how basic my teaching had to be, and also how practical. While almost all the answers I received from the presumably mature adult Bible class were correct or partially correct, every answer came short of what I had anticipated. No one, absolutely no one, came up with, "He is God."

I have asked that same question many, many times since. Seldom does anyone say, "He is God." Why, when it is so obvious from Scripture? And when most of them remarked that they knew that all the time—that is, after I give them the right answer. Is it because Christians have actually *lost the sense of the Holy Spirit being God?* Just as the Son is God? As the Father is God?

So through the years, this study has developed in very simple terms. It has assisted thousands to really understand Who the Holy Spirit is, what He does, and how He does it.

While in a special church crusade in an eastern American city I gave a message, part of which is contained in this book. As my custom is, I was staying in one of the parishioner's homes. At a light lunch late one night, my host exclaimed, "So the Holy Spirit is a person! Not only that, but He is God! Our pastor has deceived us all these years. No wonder our church is in such trouble."

The truth had finally struck home. The Holy Spirit really is God, the One who convicts, convinces, converts and consecrates. But even now the truth was not entirely clear to him. Not realizing that the Holy Spirit also came to unite, my host turned against the pastor whom he had respected and revered for a good number of years. Heart knowledge would have produced a greater love. Head knowledge produced only a resentment. (In truth, I knew the pastor had always taught the Holy Spirit to be a person. Apparently my host had a mind closed to fact.)

At a church where I was ministering in the western States, God had been restoring and reviving a congregation in desperate need of a fresh touch from heaven. Many souls were saved in the two-week period of three Sundays. Many more had been revived and were endeavoring to win the lost. And there were a few remarkable healings as well.

It was the custom of the elders in that church to meet with the pastor for prayer before each service (a practice that needs to be restored in many churches). One of the reasons the church had been so very dry was because of those praying elders. Those prayers, indeed, were vain repetitions. They said the same things every time they prayed. I already knew their prayers by heart. And each could "bathe" the world in prayer in less than thirty seconds with such utterances as, "Lord, You know the missionaries, so bless them all. Amen."

However, on the very last night of that particular campaign, one of those elders waxed very bold in prayer. He actually deviated from his usual pattern. He cried out in desperation, "Oh, God! Send it to convict us. Send it up and down the aisles, and in and out of the pews."

Instead of asking the Holy Spirit to do His work, he was asking God to send "it." Now who or what was this "it" that he was referring to? Some type of influence? A thing? Me, the evangelist? What exactly did he mean?

While I have isolated some cases by illustration, these are not isolated situations—far from it. This is far too common across the continent. And the Holy Spirit is grieved with the ignorance of God's own people. Yes, the Holy Spirit's own people.

During the very first service of special campaigns, I have heard many pastors pray something like this, "Send God to speak to us this morning." They put God in the third person, even though they are supposed to be speaking directly to Him. A complete stranger would wonder to whom the pastor was talking.

I was to introduce Dr. Dean Ortner of "Moody's Sermons from Science" to a very large Sunday morning audience in a church that by most standards would be considered solidly evangelical. They also thought they had a handle on the Holy Spirit that other churches did not have. Dean asked the pastor in charge how long he would have to give his presentation. He replied, "That depends on how long it takes me to get the spirits working."

I am not sure what he meant exactly. But I presumed that he thought it would take him a little while to get the people worked up. In other words, he had a great ignorance of the working of the Holy Spirit—both in his own life and the lives of others. It appeared to me that he was equating hyper-emotion with the moving of the Holy

Spirit. There could have been something more, of course, and we will talk about that in a later chapter.

It is my hope that this book, written in very simple English, will be used by the Holy Spirit to restore our thinking to a proper scriptural standard about the Holy Spirit Himself—Who He is, and how our actions and reactions affect His working in our lives and the life of the church.

The Holy Spirit is hurt by our ignorance. Since we are the temples in which He lives, then we too are hurting. And since we are the people who make up the Church as the Body of Christ, then we are hurting each other as we are part of that body.

Surely we need to pray anew:

Come, Holy Spirit, heavenly Dove,
    With all thy quickening powers;
Kindle a flame of sacred love
    In these cold hearts of ours.

In vain we tune our formal songs,
    In vain we strive to rise;
Hosannas languish on our tongues,
    And our devotion dies.

Dear Lord, and shall we ever live
    At this poor, dying rate?
Our love so faint, so cold, to Thee,
    And Thine to us so great?

Come, Holy Spirit, heavenly Dove,
  With all thy quickening powers;
Come, shed abroad a Saviour's love;
  And that shall kindle ours.

—Isaac Watts

Chapter 2

Ignoring Him

Yes, there is a great ignorance of who the Holy Spirit really is, even though there appears to be a greater emphasis on His work now than in many other eras of church history. This ignorance continues to prevail even though the Holy Spirit Himself has given us three continuous chapters on the subject in First Corinthians.

Many times we have to find related passages throughout the Bible to determine doctrine. But chapters 12, 13 and 14 of First Corinthians lay down principles and guidelines that ought to make it easy for anyone to know Who the Holy Spirit is and what He wants to do through us.

These three chapters begin with, "Now about spiritual gifts, brothers, I do not want you to be ignorant" (12:1). This series of chapters closes with, "If he ignores this, he himself will be ignored" (14:38).

It seems the Holy Spirit paused when He was giving us the Scriptures. He knew that the greater part of His work was to make the saving message of Christ plain to lost mankind. But at this point in Scripture, He seems to deviate a little and says in effect, "Now it is time for people to understand about Me and My work all of My work."

We get many glimpses of the Holy Spirit throughout the Old Testament especially, and some in the New Testament. But the record is piecemeal, quite unlike the picture of our Lord Jesus Christ in the eighty-nine straight chapters through the four Gospels which deal with His birth, life, ministry, death and resurrection. No place do we have anything similar about God and the Holy Spirit until we come to First Corinthians 12.

The Holy Spirit starts by saying that it is time that Christians knew about Him. He does not want us to be ignorant. But He also knows men's hearts. So He concludes that if a person insists on being ignorant well, man, by God's sovereign decree, still has his own free will. God does not take that from him.

Now ignorant contains a number of meanings in its root form. Being ignorant can mean lacking in knowledge or lacking in understanding, or both together. It can mean to be unaware of a person, message or thing. But it can mean more than that. It can also mean to have both knowledge and understanding, and simply to pay no attention to that knowledge and understanding.

In other words, we can have all the understanding that is necessary about the Holy Spirit, and choose to slight Him or disregard Him altogether. The Holy Spirit is saying that He does not want this to happen. He does not want us to be unaware of Him, but if we choose to ignore Him, that is our choice.

But the evidence of Scripture is, that when man chooses to ignore or disregard Him, He is grieved. And the Holy Spirit when grieved does not work in the church. And when the Holy Spirit does not work in a church, that same church is reduced to little more than another social club that meets on Sunday morning rather than Wednesday noon. And sometimes I think the service club might be doing a lot more than these pathetic little churches that are merely going through the motions—these churches that see no souls saved and have no positive social impact in the community. At least the service club makes a social impact.

Let us put the Holy Spirit back into proper perspective in our thinking. To do this we need to take a double look at First Corinthians 12:4-6: "There are different kinds of gifts, but the same Spirit. There are different kinds of service, but the same Lord. There are different kinds of working, but the same God works all of them in all men."

There is a pattern running through these three verses. Each of the verses has the word "diversities" or "different," both coming from the "same" Greek word. Further, we note the word same is used in each of the verses. Yes, "different" and "same," used in all three verses. This is one of the paradoxes of Scripture.

Now we are able to take the verses apart and re-construct the message in simple form. There are different gifts, administrations and operations. (This will be dealt with in the next chapter.) But there is the same Spirit, Lord and God.

At this point we want to zero in on this last thought, "The same Spirit, Lord and God." This is a very interesting sequence, inasmuch as we invariably name the Trinity in the exact opposite order as Father, Son and Holy Spirit. Generally speaking, the term "Lord" is used in the New Testament . . . to signify God the Son. And God in the New Testament generally refers to God the Father. So in this particular paragraph of Scripture we see the Trinity named in the order of Holy Spirit, Son and Father.

Notice that we are here commencing the three specific chapters that teach us more about the Holy Spirit than any other three consecutive chapters in the entire Bible. And the Holy Spirit names Himself first. Why? Might it be that we would be sure to understand that He is God, equal with the Son and with the Father? He does not do this just to prove a point, but because we continually give Him an inferior place. We do not seem to have grasped that if God is God, He is God. There cannot be a little God and a big God. God is all supreme, or He is not God.

Note again the order given here: Spirit, Son, Father.

Now let us go back to the first place in the New Testament where the Trinity is named or indicated in a single paragraph at the baptism of Jesus in the river Jordan. It is interesting that this is recorded in all four Gospels: Matthew 3:16-17, Mark 1:9-11, Luke 3:21-22 and John 1:31-34. This, of course, does not make it any more inspired than portions that are given only once. "All Scripture is God-breathed and is useful for teaching, rebuking, correcting and training in righteousness" (2 Timothy 3:16). But the repetition is for emphasis. Just as the Ten Commandments are repeated in whole or in part, many times in the Bible, so the baptism of Jesus is recorded four times for emphasis. The Holy Spirit wanted to make sure that we did not miss it on our first reading through the New Testament.

While the baptism of Jesus is recorded in all four Gospels, we will quote only from Matthew 3:16-17. "As soon as Jesus . . ." (here the Son of God is named first); ". . . was baptized, he went up out of the water. At that moment heaven was opened, and he saw the Spirit of God descending like a dove and lighting upon him" (the Holy Spirit is mentioned second); ". . . And a voice from heaven . . ." (this can be none other than God the Father. Who in this passage is indicated not first, but third); "said, 'This is my Son, whom I love; with him I am well pleased.' "

We see then, that in the first part of Matthew, the Trinity is indicated to us as the Son, the Holy Spirit and the Father. As an aid to understanding what the Holy Spirit in breathing the Scriptures is endeavoring to teach us, we will begin to construct a chart:

SCRIPTURE	FIRST NAMED	SECOND NAMED	THIRD NAMED
Matt. 3:16-17	Son	Holy Spirit	Father
1 Cor. 12:4-6	Holy Spirit	Son	Father

Now having looked at the first part of Matthew, let us look at the last part. In Matthew 28:19-20, we have not only the Great Commission, but the formula for baptism as well: "Therefore go and make disciples of all nations, baptizing them in the name of the Father and of the Son and of the Holy Spirit, and teaching them to obey everything I have commanded you. And surely I am with you always, to the very end of the age."

In part, verse nineteen is perhaps the most quoted portion of God's Word. In all denominations it is the crowning verse in the great missionary enterprise. In almost all denominations, whether evangelical, conservative or liberal, it is used at every baptismal service. How many times have you heard, "I now baptize you in the name of the Father and of the Son and of the Holy Spirit. Amen"?

This verse names the Trinity in the order of Father, Son and Holy Spirit. Because we hear this verse so very often, and know it so well, we invariably name the Trinity in this order. Thus the Father has come to be known as the First Person of the Trinity, the Son the Second Person of the Trinity and the Holy Spirit the Third Person of the Trinity.

But have we misnamed the Holy Spirit by calling Him the Third Person? And have we unconsciously given the Holy Spirit an inferior rating
because of this misnomer? I think that is part of
our problem.

Matthew 28:19 is the only verse in the entire Bible where the Trinity is named in this order.
Some will argue, "What about First John 5:7: 'For
there are three that testify: the Spirit, the water
and the blood; and the three are in agreement'?"

But First John 5:7 is really not part of God's
Word. Every Bible commentator that I have read
agrees at this point. Although this fact is accepted
by almost all Bible scholars, it is very upsetting to
many lay students who use the verse to prove the
Trinity. Therefore I have deviated from my general
plan to not quote other authors, and make this one
exception. John Stott briefly summarizes what
many other authors take pages and chapters to state:

> The whole of this verse may be regarded as
> a gloss[1]. . . .The words do not occur in any
> Greek manuscript, version or quotation be-
> fore the fifteenth century. They first appear
> in an obscure fourth-century Latin manu-
> script and found their way into the Author-
> ized Version because Erasmus reluctantly
> included them in the third edition of his
> text. They are rightly absent even from the
> margin of the Revised Version and the Re-
> vised Standard Version. Some tidy-minded
> scribe, impressed by the three-fold witness

of verse eight, must have been made to think of the Trinity and so suggested that there was a three-fold witness in heaven also. Actually his gloss is not a very happy one, as the three-fold testimony of verse eight is to Christ; and the Biblical teaching is not that the Father, Son and Holy Spirit bear witness together to the Son, but that the Father bears witness to the Son through the Spirit.[2]

We are forced by sheer fact to eliminate the only other "verse" that names the Trinity in the order of Father, Son and Holy Spirit. However, Matthew 28:19 stands with that particular order, so we are able to add Matthew 28:19-20 to our chart:

SCRIPTURE	FIRST NAMED	SECOND NAMED	THIRD NAMED
Matt. 3:16-17	Son	Holy Spirit	Father
Matt. 28:19-20	Father	Son	Holy Spirit
1 Cor. 12:4-6	Holy Spirit	Son	Father

In these three mentions of the Trinity we see three different arrangements. Let us now refer to the very last verse of Second Corinthians: "The grace of the Lord Jesus Christ, and the love of God, and the fellowship of the Holy Spirit be with you all."

A number of years ago, when I was pastoring on the eastern seaboard of Canada, I discovered that there was a graduate of one of my denomination's colleges living within easy driving distance from my church. He was pastoring a church of another denomination which held some considerably different views from what he had been taught, but I considered him a good prospect for the pastorate of the church I was starting as an outreach from my own church.

The president of my denomination at that time, Dr. Nathan Bailey, and I met with him for talks concerning this new venture. Finally, this very excellent Christian brother said to us, "There is really only one thing that keeps me from serving in the denomination of my alma mater. You fellows pretend to have fellowship with the whole Trinity, but my fellowship is with the Father and the Son, as taught in First John 1:3: '. . . And our fellowship is with the Father and with his Son, Jesus Christ.' "

Knowing a little of the conservative denomination in which he pastored and being quite quick with the tongue at the time I immediately asked, "And what benediction did you use to close your last Sunday's services?" I was taking a calculated risk.

He responded to my delight that he thought it likely was, "May the grace of the Lord Jesus Christ, and the love of God, and the fellowship of the Holy Spirit be with you all" (2 Corinthians 13:14).

"That is what I thought," I replied. "So you pray that your congregation will know the communion of the Holy Spirit, but your own communion is only with the Father and with the Son?"

The verse that he used, First John 1:3, is a good verse. It is the Bible. It is truth, but it is not all the truth. He had done what so many of God's people do. Finding one verse, they use it exclusively in spite of all the other verses that assist in giving a well-rounded biblical concept. By doing so, he eliminated the Holy Spirit from his communion even though his benediction included Him.

On the way back to our parsonage that night, Dr. Bailey calmly remarked, "Well, Bob, you certainly won your point tonight." I was delighted that he had noticed. "But in winning your point, you lost your friend and our prospect." I sat soberly through the rebuke and then thanked him for it. It is a truth that I have never forgotten. When you win an argument, you lose a friend. In winning, you become the loser. That is the hard way of discovering that the Holy Spirit is very gracious. If we allow Him to rule us, we too will be gracious.

Nevertheless, Second Corinthians 13:14 is just as good for individuals as it is for congregations. It is also a verse that helps us to build our chart:

SCRIPTURE	FIRST NAMED	SECOND NAMED	THIRD NAMED
Matt.3:16-17	Son	Holy Spirit	Father
Matt. 28:19-20	Father	Son	Holy Spirit
1 Cor.12:4-6	Holy Spirit	Son	Father
2 Cor.13:14	Son	Father	Holy Spirit

To this point our chart includes four of six possible sequences of the persons of the Trinity. Ephesians names or indicates the Trinity a number of times, each a duplication of one of three of the above orders. It is interesting, but not crucial, that Ephesians uses the orders that are used by us the least. That is right—what the Bible uses the most, we use the least. And what the Bible uses the least, we use the most.

Ephesians 2:18 tells us, "For through him we both have access to the Father by one Spirit." Here we see the order: Son, Spirit and the Father, which is a duplication of Matthew 3:16-17.

"Father we come to you in Jesus' name as the Holy Spirit gives us liberty." That is good praying. But one should not use this verse as a basis for such praying. This verse is the basis for our salvation, for both Jews and Gentiles.

Further on in Ephesians we have a duplication of the order already recognized in First Corinthians 12 actually two duplications. Ephesians 4:4-6 tells us, "There is one body and one Spirit—just as you were called to one hope when you were called—one Lord, one faith, one baptism; one God and Father of all, who is over all and through all and in all." Then in the next chapter we read, "Do not get drunk on wine, which leads to debauchery. Instead, be filled with the Spirit. Speak to one another with psalms, hymns and spiritual songs. Sing and make music in your heart to the Lord, always giving thanks to God the Father for everything, in the name of our Lord Jesus Christ" (Ephesians 5:18-20).

In these two paragraphs from two different chapters, we have the same sequence: Holy Spirit, Son and the Father, making three different times out of the seven verses quoted that the Trinity is named in this particular order. The order is exactly opposite to that which we almost invariably use.

We turn next to First Peter 1:2 where we read, "who have been chosen according to the foreknowledge of God the Father, through the sanctifying work of the Spirit, for obedience to Jesus Christ and sprinkling by his blood: Grace and peace be yours in abundance." Here again, we see the Trinity revealed in one select verse. We often lose sight of this by getting so involved in the great areas of controversy contained in the verse: election, foreknowledge and sanctification. What a verse! What a mind Peter must have had! He just writes it as though we would all be able to understand without explanation.

But for our study we will simply use the verse to note an addition to our chart. I am adding the verses simply as we come to them in the Bible. The order of the verses is not significant, although later on we will see that sometimes the order given does have some special importance.

Our chart now looks like this:

SCRIPTURE	FIRST NAMED	SECOND NAMED	THIRD NAMED
Matt. 3:16-17	Son	Holy Spirit	Father
Matt. 28:19-20	Father	Son	Holy Spirit
1 Cor. 12:4-6	Holy Spirit	Son	Father
2 Cor. 13:14	Son	Father	Holy Spirit
1 Peter 1:2	Father	Holy Spirit	Son

That leaves us with one more sequence to find. It is in the tiny book of Jude. Now this little book of Jude has some very interesting and exciting words from God. Included in this is the last paragraph in the Bible that mentions all the persons of the Godhead by name: "But you, dear friends, build yourselves up in your most holy faith and pray in the Holy Spirit. Keep yourselves in God's love as you wait for the mercy of our Lord Jesus Christ to bring you to eternal life" (Jude 20-21).

Here we see the Godhead named individually as God the Holy Spirit, God the Father and God the Son. This is sufficient now to finish our chart. Remember that there is no significance in the order that I have printed them. Our final chart looks like this:

SCRIPTURE	FIRST NAMED	SECOND NAMED	THIRD NAMED
Matt. 3:16-17	Son	Holy Spirit	Father
Matt. 28:19-20	Father	Son	Holy Spirit
1 Cor. 12:4-6	Holy Spirit	Son	Father
2 Cor. 13:14	Son	Father	Holy Spirit
1 Peter 1:2	Father	Holy Spirit	Son
Jude 20-21	Holy Spirit	Father	Son

We have now seen that each sequence of names of the Trinity is used at least once in the Scriptures. I have purposely used a number of pages to show this. It is something that we need to take in and thoroughly digest. We need to restore our thinking on Who the Trinity really is. Notice from the chart that not one of the Persons of the Godhead is given special priority. Why is it then that so many people single out one of the Trinity and almost completely try to avoid the others?

The very fact that children generally refer to the Holy Spirit as God, but adults very often refer to Him as "it," is sufficient reason for us older Christians to reflect on what has happened not to our theology, but to our thinking.

We have unconsciously delegated the Holy Spirit to an inferior level. This has happened even in fellowships where there may seem to be an overemphasis on the Holy Spirit. In these circles we hear such phrases as, "Have you got it yet?" and "Don't do anything. Just tarry until you get it," and further, "Wait for it to happen." The emphasis is on the gift and not the Giver, and the Giver is reduced to a thing or an influence, when indeed, He is a person.

This is aptly illustrated by an incident in my home church in Ontario. I was teaching a group of young people about the Trinity, and I was looking for something that would be practical for the students to use if they should be called upon to give a similar study. It so happened that in designing the building the architect decided to light the sanctuary by hanging "little trinities" from the Swiss ceiling. The building being quite sizeable, it was necessary to have many of these lighting fixtures of three frosted globes each. Each fixture had a small globe at the top and a large one at the bottom. A medium-sized one hung at the intermediate level completing each triangular setting.

I asked these youths to explain how we could use this lighting arrangement to teach boys and girls about God. One young man ventured immediately, "It can't be done. God the Father would be represented by the big one, so it should be on the top, not at the bottom. The little globe should be on the bottom because it would represent the Holy Spirit. The middle-sized one is okay in the middle because it could stand for Jesus."

You see what we have unconsciously done? We have slowly but surely delegated the Holy Spirit to be the little fellow at the bottom. We give Him the basement apartment. He is the One that does not matter much in our thinking. This is my general observation through over forty years of ministry as a pastor and then as an evangelist.

Now we must not start calling Him the First Person of the Trinity, nor the Second. To change our terminology would only cause confusion. I am not calling for a change of title for the Holy Spirit, but rather I am calling for a change of attitude by Christendom at large. We need to keep our terminology, but not allow our terminology to delegate the Holy Spirit to an inferior position.

I have often asked three questions as I have traveled extensively in the United States: 1) Who is the first lady of America? 2) Who is the second lady? and 3) Who is the third lady? Almost everyone has known the first lady by her first name, whether it has been in the Kennedy, Johnson, Nixon, Ford, Carter, Reagan, Bush or Clinton eras. The answer to the second question is a little harder to come by. Most people know her as Mrs. if they know her at all. With a little coaxing, I am sometimes able to get her first name, but very seldom. But only once have I had a group where more than one person could give me even the last name of the third lady of the United States. Generally, no one knows at all, not even her last name. And some do not even know that a third lady exists.

Note the inference: First persons are important enough to know by their first names. Second persons are not so important. And third persons are not important at all. It appears that we have unconsciously done this to the Holy Spirit. Forever referring to Him as the Third Person of the Trinity, we have slowly taught our people that He does not count for much. Such a deadly error! Churches that ignore the Holy Spirit soon begin to ignore Jesus Christ as Savior and Lord, and the general term "God" is later used to signify just about anything they want it to.

I have asked many why we think so lowly of the Holy Spirit. One time I received a classic answer that rather sums up what so many have said. A lady of very fine education, both secular and Christian, stated, "It is because there is nothing about Him at all in the Old Testament, and He does not come into being until the Day of Pentecost."

To answer this, I had the audience turn to the very first verses of the Bible where we read, "In the beginning God created the heavens and the earth. Now the earth was formless and empty, darkness was over the surface of the deep, and the Spirit of God was hovering over the waters" (Genesis 1:1-2). Here we see the Holy Spirit in operation, and being mentioned by name before the Father and the Son. You see, the word used here for God is plural in the Hebrew, denoting at least three. Therefore, in verse one the word "God" must refer to the entire Trinity.

A well-educated man, thinking on a completely secular basis, offered this, "In order to have a son, you must first have a father. Then I suppose, together they were able to produce a special spirit." "Then," I said, "we might have a little difficulty with the Christmas story which tells us about the Holy Spirit ministering to Mary before Jesus was born." This brought gales of laughter. It also opened the group to a very interesting discussion. It also prepared the group for some of my teaching on the Holy Spirit in the Old Testament which we deal with later in this book.

Let us restore the Holy Spirit in our thinking to His proper place: one with the Father, and one with the Son. This is what the Holy Spirit Himself is trying to say to us when He states, ". . . brothers, I do not want you to be ignorant" (1 Corinthians 12:1).

But being ignorant, we grieve Him. It would be fitting if we all could pray:

Holy Ghost, with light divine,
  Shine upon this heart of mine;
Chase the shades of night away;
  Turn my darkness into day.

Holy Ghost, with power divine,
  Cleanse this guilty heart of mine;
Long hath sin, without control,
  Held dominion o'er my soul.

Holy Ghost, with joy divine,
  Cheer this saddened heart of mine;
Bid my many woes depart;
  Heal my wounded, bleeding heart.

Holy Spirit, all divine,
  Dwell within this heart of mine;
Cast down every idol throne;
  Reign supreme—and reign alone.

— Andrew Reed

Endnotes

1. A gloss is an explanation inserted between the lines of a text to clarify a foreign or difficult word; or a translation inserted between the lines of a text printed in a foreign language.
2. John R.W. Stott, *The Epistle of John, Tyndale New Testament Commentaries* (Grand Rapids, MI: William B. Eerdmans Publishing Company, 1979), 180.

Chapter 3

There Is a Difference

In the previous chapter we dealt with the "same" element of the "same/different" paradox of First Corinthians 12:4-6. Now let us look at the different gifts . . . administrations . . . operations.

At the outset, we might well ask ourselves three questions: What are *gifts*? What are *administrations*? And what are *workings*? Unless these are clear, the student of God's Word will become confused and go astray in his studies.

There is confusion as people endeavor to answer these three questions. Gifts are many times equated with talents and graces. So in this chapter, we want to distinguish between gifts, talents and graces. We will also distinguish between gifts, administrations and operations. Then we will see the relative value of the gifts in our own ministries.

The Apostle Paul was writing to the Corinthian church, a group of people who professed to know Jesus Christ as Savior and Lord. The fact that Paul was dealing with gross sin in the congregation does not alter the fact that he was writing to the church. Nor do his closing remarks in the second epistle to the Corinthians alter this fact: "Examine yourselves to see whether you are in the faith; test yourselves" (2 Corinthians 13:5).

Let us remember that Paul was not only addressing himself to some very unfortunate circumstances at Corinth—he is addressing himself to us as well. This is God speaking through Paul to all of us as part of the Church of Jesus Christ. And remember further that these three chapters concerning the Holy Spirit are dealing with our ignorance. They are not dealing with the other issues in the epistle that are given in order as disunity, immorality, stinginess and heresy. No—these three chapters deal almost entirely with our ignorance of the workings of the Holy Spirit.

Further, many Christians endeavor to equate the gifts of the Holy Spirit with any kind of gift. This has been a natural evolution. Instead of being specific in our conversation, we have so often spoken of "gifts" rather than the more precise "gifts of the Holy Spirit." Thus when we talk about a Christian being gifted, we have not indicated whether that same person is musical or whether he is filled with faith. The former is a talent. The latter is a gift of the Holy Spirit. More properly we should say that the Christian musician is talented rather than gifted. But he may be gifted as well, if he is filled with the Holy Spirit.

Let us note again that Paul is writing to professing Christians, the Church. This is not for everyone. It is not for those outside the Body of Christ. He is talking about things that Christians can receive from the Holy Spirit: "Now about spiritual gifts [things], brothers . . ." (1 Corinthians 12:1). They are not things that the unsaved are likely to possess. Many unsaved people outshine Christians in talents, but the gifts of the Holy Spirit are for Christians only.

Further, the Christian can know and needs to know what his special gift of the Holy Spirit is. And he may have many gifts. It appears the Apostle Paul may have had them all. To make it easier for us to know what the gifts are, Paul has named almost every one of them very conveniently in Romans twelve and First Corinthians twelve. Of course, some of these are mentioned in other places as well, but we need go little further than these two chapters.

First Corinthians 12:7 tells us, "Now to each one the manifestation of the Spirit is given for the common good." Since the Holy Spirit is writing to Christians, He is telling us in effect that every Christian needs to know the manifestation of the Holy Spirit, so that the whole church can be benefited.

Now we are not to allow one verse of Scripture to form the whole foundation for an argument or doctrine. One sentence is not to be isolated from what is elsewhere taught in the Scriptures. Let us compare, therefore, First Corinthians 12:11: "All these are the work of one and the same Spirit, and he gives them to each one, just as he determines."

We are now able to see that verses 7 and 11 have a phrase that is common to each. It is "to each one;" that is, to every Christian. It is so simple to see if we line these verses up congruently:

VERSE 7:	the manifestation of the Spirit is given to every man
VERSE 11:	the very same Spirit dividing to every man . . .

In other words, the Holy Spirit has a manifestation of Himself to give to every one of His children.

Ephesians 4:7-8, 11 supports this: "But to each one of us grace has been given as Christ apportioned it. This is why it says: 'When he ascended up on high, he led captives in his train and gave gifts to men.' . . . It was he who gave some to be apostles, some to be prophets, some to be evangelists, and some to be pastors and teachers; . . ."

Now if you were asked to write down in black and white what your gift for ministry is, would you be able to do so? If not, why not? And if not, how do you know where you fit into the body of Christ for ministry to individuals and to the Church as a whole? That many Christians do not know what their gift is, is one of the reasons many feel completely out of place in the area of service in which they find themselves. They may be in the wrong area of service altogether.

While pastoring a number of years ago, one of the elders of my church brought up what he considered to be a problem at our regular elders' meeting. The teacher of the junior teen Sunday school class of boys had not been attending the midweek prayer meeting with any degree of regularity. My very negative elder thought that he should not be allowed to teach if this circumstance prevailed. It appeared that the other elders would be swayed by this one elder.

When I asked the elders what particular gift of the Holy Spirit would be necessary to pray effectively, it was agreed that it would be the gift of faith. Then I asked, "And what gift of the Spirit is necessary to be able to be a good Sunday school teacher?"

Very reluctantly one elder ventured almost sarcastically, "I suppose you are expecting us to say, 'the gift of teaching.'"

"Right!" I responded. "And it appears to me that this man has the gift of teaching." (This I knew in part because I had two sons in the class under question, and they were quite keen about their teacher.)

Another elder supported me with, "And my son actually looks forward to his classes and his special outings as well."

The case would have been dropped immediately if I had not continued it. "This man makes his living, and his ministry possible, by selling insurance. If he were to take time away from his selling to attend every weeknight service, he might go bankrupt. Then we would accuse him of not having God's blessing and again bring in a resolution to take away his class. Besides, brethren, it appears to me that he has the gift of giving as well as the gift of teaching."

I pressed a little further. "In addition to the many qualifications in First Timothy 3 and Titus 1, there are two gifts of the Spirit that are necessary for a person to qualify as a lay leader. Do you know what they are?"

One elder responded, "I didn't even know there were qualifications let alone special gifts of the Holy Spirit. What are they?"

I read them the account from Acts where the first lay leaders were set apart for a certain ministry by the apostles and the church at Jerusalem. " 'Brothers, choose seven men from among you who are known to be full of the Spirit and wisdom. We will turn this responsibility over to them. . . .' This proposal pleased the whole group. They chose Stephen, a man full of faith and of the Holy Spirit. . . .So the word of God spread. The number of disciples in Jerusalem increased rapidly . . ." (Acts 6:3-7).

These new spiritual leaders were to be filled with the Holy Spirit, especially manifesting the two gifts of wisdom and faith. Thus I emphasized to my board that each one needed to know the Holy Spirit in a very personal way. They, too, were to have the two gifts of wisdom and faith. Wisdom would assist them in knowing what needed to be accomplished in the Church and how to accomplish it. Faith was needed so each of them could trust God for the *doing* until it was done.

I explained to them the three methods the church has used to fill positions of service. The

first was the *consecration* method—if you loved the
Lord sincerely, you were thought to be able to do
anything in the church and it would work. Mistaken use of this method is one of the reasons for
burnout in the ministry.

Then there is the *gifts* method. If you show that
you are able to do something well, you are asked
to do it even if you are not living a consecrated
life.

Then there is the *consecration-gifts* method. This
is what the Lord is able to bless. When the dedication of Shadrach, Meshach and Abednego is cou-
pled with the gift of the Holy Spirit that enables
us for the task, then there is success. Remember
that the three Hebrew children said that God was
able to deliver them from the burning furnace, but
if He decided not to, it made little difference to
them. They would love Him just the same. That
is commitment. It is not "I will serve you, Lord, if
You do such and such."

The matter of the gifts will be dealt with more
fully later. The above, however, will serve to show
us what the gifts of the Holy Spirit are—special
functions from the Holy Spirit given to Christians
for service, as the Holy Spirit desires that person
to have, and knows that that is what is needed.

Let us next see the word *administration* (1 Corinthians 12:5). Today the word indicates a person
who has the oversight of a task or group of people,
an administrator. But the word here more rightly
should be translated "ministries" as is shown in
the margin of most King James Version editions

of the Bible. It is translated as "services" or "ministries" in most new versions.

This designates the type of service that the Christian enters into by the grace of God. He may have the gift of teaching, but he does not enter into the ministry of teaching until he begins to teach. It has to be a service unto the Lord that affects others. Without the enduement from the Holy Spirit, his teaching is only a job, not a ministry.

A person may have the gift of showing mercy or compassion. That ministry only begins, however, when that person begins to show compassion to another person in the name of Jesus Christ. Such a person could even have worked as a nurse, for example, but only as a job rather than as a ministry in the name of Christ.

We turn now to *operations*, as indicated in First Corinthians 12:6. When we use the word *operations* today, we immediately think of a surgeon applying his skills in the operating room to restore someone's body. This picture can be carried over into the Christian sphere of life as well. Indeed, the word refers to the way in which the Christian will use his God-given talents or skills to minister to the Body of Christ. However, to more correctly suit the word to today's English, it should be translated "workings" or "ways of doing things."

Quite early in my ministry, I was appointed, sight unseen, to a church that had previously been pastored by two single ladies. The older of the two lived in a small cottage right on the church property and continued to do so after my arrival. I was about half her age and quite newly married. My wife and I lived in an apartment in the church building. The older single lady did not approve of the way in which this very young married man endeavored to use his gift of pastoring. And the inverse was also true. There was tension.

Now either person's method may have been correct. It was only the tension that was wrong. The problem arose when two people, with perhaps the same gifts, having the same ministry, used different ways to accomplish an end.

This should not have been a problem at all. It should have been recognized as a blessing. How humdrum this world would be if we all did things exactly alike. This oversight has been the cause of much contention in the Church down through the years. We need to recognize the different gifts, ministries and ways, as indeed Paul did. As indeed, the Holy Spirit does. And unfortunately, as the Corinthian church did not. And as many of us do not.

There need not be a great problem just because two personalities clash. Those same two personalities can be used to augment each other's ministries by supporting each other, rather than tearing down. Then, too, if somebody is "stroking us the wrong way," it might be a good idea to simply turn around.

After I learned some very hard lessons as a young pastor, I discovered I should always be willing to take the humble place, even when I thought I was right. Having moved from the west coast of Canada to the east coast, I soon lost the whereabouts of the lady pastor mentioned above. But after thirty years I was able to visit her in a nursing home in Calgary, AB. I apologized for the way I had responded to her, back in the fifties. She was delighted to see me, accepted my apology and forgave. Needless to say, we had a little camp meeting even though it was winter.

Let us remember that the gifts of the Holy Spirit are not talents. Talents are those things that both the saved and the unsaved may have. They are abilities to do things. A talent, therefore, can be carpentry, singing, playing an instrument, being a mechanic, typing, craftsmanship, cooking, pottery making, jack-of-all-trades, etc. It is an inborn ability that can be cultivated. Or it may simply be a learned process.

My wife, Gwen, is a gifted vibraharpist. She not only plays accompaniments, but also the very difficult solos, for which she creates her own arrangements. One night in Truro, Nova Scotia, during the ministry of evangelist Clarence Shrier, she recognized her need of being filled with the Spirit and knowing it, instead of merely being a temple of the Holy Spirit where He casually resided.

The next night as she played her vibraharp just before the message, people began to come to the altar. The message had not even started. God had begun to speak through her music. Before, she performed. Now, she ministers.

Just as we should not confuse the gifts of the Holy Spirit with our talents, so we should not confuse the gifts of the Holy Spirit with the graces of the Holy Spirit. These latter are known as "the fruit of the Spirit." There are nine of these graces lumped together and called one fruit. Notice the singular, "But the fruit of the Spirit is love, joy, peace, patience, kindness, goodness, faithfulness, gentleness and self-control . . ." (Galatians 5:22-23).

Now it appears that many Christians, whether laity or clergy, do not agree with this assertion of one fruit instead of nine fruits. This is quite evident from the continuous use of their terminology, "fruits of the Spirit."

However, the Bible is plain at this point: "The fruit of the Spirit is . . ."—singular. I have at least twenty-eight versions and translations of the Bible in my library. They are all translated in the singular; there is no excuse for using the plural, "fruits." Yes, it is one fruit—with nine sections or flavors.

Each one of these graces by itself is merely a personality trait that may be seen in either the Christian or non-Christian. That is one reason why all nine flavors lumped together are called one fruit. The Spirit-filled saint will not have just one or two of these graces, but all nine of them. This one fruit with its nine flavors is one of the evidences of the Spirit-filled life. If any of the flavors is missing, it is an evidence that we do not have the fruit, because that one fruit contains all the flavors.

Now I want to chart the gifts of the Spirit, the graces or fruit of the Spirit and the talents that we might have. In this way we will be helped to bear in mind that there is a difference between these three designations.

Gifts of the Spirit (1 Corinthians 12:8-10)	Fruit of the Spirit (Galatians 5:22-23)	Talents (non biblical list)
Word of wisdom	Love	Musician
Word of knowledge	Joy	Carpenter
Faith	Peace	Physician
Gifts of healing	Long-suffering	Cook
Working of miracles	Gentleness	Caretaker
Prophecy	Goodness	Mechanic
Discerning of spirits	Faith	Typist
Kinds of tongues	Meekness	Welder
Interpretation of tongues	Self-control	Singer

The list of the flavors of the fruit of the Spirit is complete. The other two are merely representative of much longer lists. If the list for the gifts of the Spirit and the list for the talents were extended, they would include teaching, which is both a talent and a special gift from the Holy Spirit. In other words, both the saved and the unsaved person are able to teach, but for the Christian there is the gift of teaching from the Holy Spirit as well. This enables that endowed person to not only have a job, but also to have a ministry.

As the lists stand, there is already one duplication. Faith is seen to be both a gift of the Holy Spirit and a grace of the Holy Spirit. Of course it could be argued that *faith* in Galatians 5:22 could be translated as "faithfulness." This is true, but it is impossible to have real faithfulness without some kind of faith. Faithfulness involves loyalty, and it would be very difficult to be loyal to somebody or something without having faith in that person or thing.

Having seen all of this, what can we say about the lethargic church of today? God has given us the possibility of many gifts. There are so many talents and talented people. The graces or fruit of the Spirit are so beautiful. There are so many ministries we can have as individuals and groups. And there are so many ways to do all these ministries. How is it that so little is accomplished for our Lord Jesus Christ? Why is it that so many churches have remained so very small for so many years?

One reason is that some denominations press only for consecration ministries and end up with misfits doing the wrong thing in the wrong place. They are square pegs trying to fit into round holes.

Another reason is the swing to gift ministries. In this, people who are gifted, whether by the Holy Spirit or by talents, are pressed into service without any degree of thought about right living. This way we end up with churches like the one at Corinth.

What is needed is a combination of the two: consecration-gift ministries. To bring about this kind of ministry, the church determines what gifts certain people have, trains them for their minis-

tries to develop these gifts and uses them only
when they have attained a degree of dedication to
the task that will keep them going ahead in the
service of the King of kings and Lord of lords.

One of my pastor friends was asked to be the special speaker at the sixtieth anniversary of a certain
church. Though meetings were originally planned
for a whole week, they were eventually trimmed
down to a weekend of services, commencing Friday
evening and concluding Sunday night.

(This is an unfortunate practice today. A study
of special campaigns will quickly reveal the
greater value of the longer series of one or more
weeks of meetings. The Word of God quickens.
Many people get no more of God's Word than
what they get on Sunday morning. If we would
get back to the long series of meetings, these people would likely manage to get out to a few of the
meetings along the way, and the church would
have the possibility of being revived. In Acts 20,
Paul talks about meetings that continued for one
week, another for three months, and even one that
lasted for three years "night and day.")

Then the Saturday night sixtieth anniversary
banquet had to be canceled. The women of the
church could not decide what to serve without
getting embroiled in deep argument. The eight
days of meetings were now reduced to a meeting
on Friday night and the regular Sunday services.

Thirty attended Sunday school that weekend.
There were thirty-one at the morning worship
service and only twenty-eight at the evening evan-

gel. That is approximately one-half a person per year in the history of the church.

This is certainly no reflection on the guest speaker who had a very successful pastorate at the time and continues to have to this day. But the church has subsequently been closed. Why? A number of ministers who pastored that church left the ministry. Why? Is there an adequate reason for this, when a church is surrounded by unchurched people? It is obvious that there was no moving of the Holy Spirit in the church. The Holy Spirit must have been sorely grieved to withdraw His blessing almost completely from a local body of believers.

"My brothers, this should not be" (James 3:10). The Lord has given us all the equipment necessary, both spiritually and physically, to do the job.

We need to "seek first his kingdom and his righteousness, and all these things will be given to you as well" (Matthew 6:33). Further, "Ask and it will be given to you; seek and you will find; knock and the door will be opened to you. . . . Which of you fathers, if your son asks for a fish, will give him a snake instead? Or if he asks for an egg, will give him a scorpion? If you then, though you are evil, know how to give good gifts to your children, how much more will your Father in heaven give the Holy Spirit to those who ask him!" (Luke 11:9-13).

Let us ask:

Hover o'er me, Holy Spirit,
  Bathe my trembling heart and brow;

Fill me with Thy hallowed presence;
   Come, oh, come and fill me now.
Thou canst fill me, gracious Spirit,
   Though I cannot tell Thee how;
But I need Thee, greatly need Thee;
   Come, oh, come and fill me now.

I am weakness, full of weakness—
   At Thy sacred feet I bow;
Blest, divine, eternal Spirit,
   Fill with power, and fill me now.

Cleanse and comfort, bless and save me;
   Bathe, oh, bathe my heart and brow;
Thou art comforting and saving,
   Thou art sweetly filling now.

Fill me now, fill me now,
   Jesus, come and fill me now.
Fill me with Thy hallowed presence;
   Come, oh, come and fill me now.

—Elwood H. Stokes

Chapter 4

The Best Gifts

Some ardent students of the Word contend that there are thirty-three different gifts of the Holy Spirit. More conservative ones say there are twenty-three or twenty-four. There are those who find only seventeen. Some in my classes have ventured forth with nine as their first guess.

Why is there such a wide range of opinions? The answer is quite simple. For example, some scholars link together the gift of ruling with the gift of governments. They state that these are one and the same. Others emphatically say "no" to this alignment.

Then there are those who deviate from the general practice of using only the larger lists of the gifts such as that in First Corinthians 12. They include other gifts whether they are designated in the Scriptures as gifts of the Holy Spirit or not. For example, some include the interpreting of dreams and visions, Joseph and Daniel generally given as examples. Joseph and Daniel are ignored by other scholars completely. Still others say that since this is in the Old Testament, it is not relevant to our times.

I have a very difficult time accepting that argument. I believe God's Word to be God's Word whether written by a prophet 5,000 years ago or 2,000 years ago. When God says, "I the LORD do not change" (Malachi 3:6), I believe that is exactly what He means. Interestingly enough, the Holy Spirit gave us this verse in the last book of the Old Testament, as He was preparing us to accept the New Testament.

Further, dreams or visions did not terminate with the ending of the Old Testament. The prophecy of Joel is repeated in Acts 2:17, "In the last days, God says, I will pour out my Spirit on all people. Your sons and daughters will prophesy, your young men will see visions, your old men will dream dreams."

Remember, too, that Pilate's wife had been warned in a dream concerning the trial of Jesus. When Pilate "was sitting on the judge's seat, his wife sent him this message: 'Don't have anything to do with that innocent man, for I have suffered a great deal today in a dream because of him'" (Matthew 27:19).

Of visions, I need only say that they are mentioned and used as direction in service six times in Acts 9 through Acts 11, eleven times elsewhere in the New Testament, and eighty-three times in the Old Testament.

But we need to be very careful concerning dreams and visions. We can make them say almost anything we want them to say. And that is the terrible danger of being steered by something so vague, rather than by the Word of God. And if the dream or vision opposes biblical teachings, you may be sure that it is not from God at all.

I had just returned to a church for a second crusade within two years. Almost immediately a lady who had sought the Lord during the first crusade approached me. I had cautioned her previously concerning a certain group with whom she had loosely associated herself.

On this occasion, she began to tell me how God had answered her prayers in my brief absence. "God has called me to be an evangelist," she declared.

"That is just marvelous," I responded. "That means your husband has become a Christian."

"No. My husband has not become a Christian," she retorted. "And what has that got to do with it?"

"That has a lot to do with it," I said. "If your husband is not saved, it is not likely that you will take him with you on your evangelistic crusades. And if he has not become a Christian, the Bible says that you cannot leave him behind. Therefore you are stuck with staying at home and being a good wife until he does get saved." I quoted First Corinthians 7:13 to her: "And if a woman has a husband who is not a believer and he is willing to live with her, she must not divorce him."

"I don't care," she replied. "A little bluebird lit on my shoulder and told me to leave him to become an evangelist, and I'm doing it."

I warned her that she had better trust in God who had spoken in His Word rather than trust a vision or dream or actual experience of having a bird speak to her.

"The bird evidently spoke lies and not the truth," I declared. With that she stomped away in anger.

But accounts of such delusions do not prove that dreams are not for us today. These incidents only serve to show the dangers.

Nevertheless, God did not change His mind between the Old and the New Testaments. Such arguments, as believed by many, that the Holy Spirit *fills* people in the dispensation of grace, but only *came upon* people in the dispensation of law, do not hold up under the illumination of the Scriptures.

It is true that the Holy Spirit came upon Samson, Othniel, Saul, Balaam and a host of others to do great exploits on certain occasions. But what about Evan Roberts in the great Welsh revival? It appears that the Holy Spirit did the same thing with him when he was only twenty-six years of age. He had been a coal miner and blacksmith almost right up until the time that God began using him mightily. Although the effects of the revival were felt for many years, Evan Roberts dropped into obscurity almost as soon as the great public meetings terminated.

We can easily see that we must not isolate cases and verses and form our doctrines and beliefs without looking at both sides of the argument. Let us take a look at the other side.

In the Old Testament people were indeed filled with the Holy Spirit as well as simply anointed for a specific situation. The garment makers in Exodus 28:3 (KJV), were "filled with the spirit of wisdom, that they may make Aaron's garments to consecrate him."

Then there was the craftsman Bezalel, the grandson of Hur of the tribe of Judah. God told Moses, "I have filled him with the Spirit of God, with skill, ability and knowledge in all kinds of crafts" (Exodus 31:3). Bezalel was not one of God's great prophets; he was a man who made things. It is repeated of him, "See, the LORD has chosen Bezalel . . . and he has filled him with the Spirit of God, with skill, ability and knowedge in all kinds of crafts" (Exodus 35:30-31).

In Numbers 27:18, Moses was told to "Take Joshua son of Nun, a man in whom is the spirit, and lay your hand on him." Further on we are told, "Joshua the son of Nun was full of the spirit of wisdom: for Moses had laid his hands upon him" (Deuteronomy 34:9, KJV). Moses must have been filled himself in order for this to happen.

Note concerning Joshua that the Holy Spirit lived within him. Then when Moses laid his hands upon him, he was filled. One might argue that if Moses knew of such happenings, why does he not tell us about his own experience of being filled? Ah! Here is a truth that is grossly over-looked today. People who are genuinely filled with the Holy Spirit do not go around telling of their experience. Rather they tell about Jesus. Jesus Himself told His followers in His last earthly appearance to them, "But you will receive power when the Holy Spirit comes on you; and you will be my witnesses . . ." (Acts 1:8).

It is quite possible that the Holy Spirit is grieved by some well-meaning people who have really had a special Holy Spirit experience. Some insist that they tell of these experiences only to other Christians, instead of telling the gospel of Christ to non-Christians. It could be one reason why some who profess to be Spirit-filled are sometimes so troublesome. They repel instead of draw. But the Holy Spirit draws people. He does not repel—He is not repulsive.

There are people who very quickly recognize the gift or gifts of the Spirit in their lives. The Spirit bears witness to their spirits. "And it is the Spirit who testifies, because the Spirit is truth" (1 John 5:6), and "The Spirit himself testifies with our spirit . . ." (Romans 8:16).

The Spirit often works through the Church to confirm the presence of gifts in individual Christians. The church either affirms or disavows what we believe to be a gift of the Holy Spirit working in our lives. This is a part of ministering one to another.

This method practically eliminates what some term the gift of martyrdom as being a gift of the Spirit. If a gift is to be affirmed by the church, it must be exercised. If the church decided that you did not have the so-called gift of martyrdom after you tried it once, it would be forever too late!

Further, the gifts are something that you employ, not what somebody else employs on you. This may sound trite or even sarcastic. However, many believe martyrdom to be a gift of the Spirit, so I have taken time to show that such is impossible.

There is also the matter of singleness. Should this be added to the list of gifts? Or is it a talent, or a ministry or a way of doing a job? If we term it a gift of the Spirit, then we might have to include marriage as well. But since marriage is quite the opposite of singleness, we would have to then conclude that it is the opposite to being a gift of the Spirit—that is, if singleness really is a gift of the Spirit.

We do get into some real difficulty, do we not, when we endeavor to stretch the gifts of the Holy Spirit into areas that the Bible itself refuses to designate?

With these cautions in mind, we can still be certain that when the Holy Spirit Himself labels certain things as gifts from Himself to Christians, then they are gifts of the Holy Spirit indeed.

The Spirit tells us to "eagerly desire the greater gifts . . ." (1 Corinthians 12:31). Now this could mean the best gifts for us in our particular ministries. Indeed, the best gifts for us would be the ones that make it possible for us to have the most successful ministry in the sphere of service to which the Holy Spirit has called us.

Some may not be aware the Holy Spirit is that person of the Godhead who calls us to particular tasks. It was Jesus who said, "Ask the Lord of the harvest, therefore, to send out workers into his harvest field" (Matthew 9:38). The identity of the Lord of the Harvest is made clear by such verses as: "While they were worshiping the Lord and fasting, the Holy Spirit said, 'Set apart for me Barnabas and Saul for the work to which I have called them.' . . . The two of them, sent on their way by the Holy Spirit, went down to Seleucia . . ." (Acts 13:2-4).

So the Holy Spirit called Saul and Barnabas, separated them for the work and sent them forth. This is the answer to the prayer that Jesus designated. Much dryness has resulted in the churches because the Holy Spirit is completely ignored when we are asking the "Lord of the harvest to send out workers."

But there is more to the meaning of "best gifts" than what we have stated. Paul does say that there are some gifts that are best, but he does not exactly label them, although he does compare a few. I suppose it would not have seemed the better part of valor for Paul to say, "Apostleship is the best gift, and I happen to have it."

When we take a look at First Corinthians 14:5, we certainly can see that there is indication of good, better and best overall: "He who prophesies is greater than one who speaks in tongues, unless he interprets, so that the church may be edified." Here Paul is saying that prophecy is a better gift than tongues. But he is also saying that if you have both tongues and interpretation of tongues, the two combined are at least of the same value as prophecy.

There is another way to show that the gifts are designated in order of value and importance—that is, to present them in chart form. But a note of caution must precede what I am about to do. Just because the Bible begins with Genesis 1:1, and ends with Revelation 22:21, it does not follow that Genesis 1:1 is more important than Revelation 22:21. Simply naming something first does not necessarily mean it is better.

It is entirely impossible for the Bible to be written in order of importance. It is all completely important. Every verse, yes, every word and every letter would have to be printed on top of each other, if it were to be written in order of importance.

Yet there can be trends. When something is repeated over and over again in the same sequence, there is likely an indication of succession of importance or authority.

When we consider the lists of gifts, some of them are named in a particular order every time. Is the Holy Spirit trying to say something to us, especially in the light of our examination of First Corinthians 14:5 and 12:31 concerning the values of the gifts. Not that there are any poor gifts— they are all good gifts. But there is an indication that some are better than others, and there are the best ones as well.

Nobody, absolutely nobody, has the right to tell another Christian that he is inferior because

he has a seemingly lesser gift. By the same to-
ken, nobody has the right to feel exalted because
he has what appears to be a better gift. It is not
likely, in fact, that the Holy Spirit would give a
person a "best gift" if he could not be trusted to
use it wisely.

I once was invited to stay at the home of a
choice Christian couple while I was attending a
convention. It was so evident that both of them
had the gift of helps. But a friend of theirs kept
begging them to really get filled with the Spirit so
they could *be something*. They needed "it" was the
claim. It is unfortunate that their friend felt supe-
rior but had no particular ministry of her own.
This is quite contrary to the Scripture which ex-
horts us, "Do nothing out of selfish ambition or
vain conceit, but in humility consider others better than yourselves" (Philippians 2:3).

With all this in mind I have charted out the gifts
of the Spirit from the lists given in the Scriptures.
There is also an addendum which includes those
classifications that some scholars include which
are not found in any of the scriptural lists. Further, although some do, I have not included the
fruit of the Spirit as I have already explained. (See
chart on next page.)

This chart needs to be examined and studied.
The order of the references has no significance. It
was simply the easiest order in which to build and
follow the chart.

Now at a glance one can readily see that a sequence is repeated. Almost without fail, the gifts

	THE GIFTS OF THE SPIRIT				
from Ephesians 4:11	from 1 Corinthians 12:28	from 1 Corinthians 12:29-30	from 1 Corinthians 12:8-10	from Romans 12:6-8	Addendum
Apostles	Apostles	Apostles	Word of wisdom		
Prophets	Prophets	Prophets	Word of knowledge	Prophecy	
Evangelists			Faith	Faith	
Pastors				Ministry	Dream interpretation
Teachers	Teachers	Teachers		Teaching	Vision interpretation
				Exhortation	Hospitality
	Miracles	Workers of miracles	Gifts of healing		Singleness
	Gifts of healings	Gifts of healing	Working of miracles	Giving	Martyrdom
					Writing
			Prophecy		Peacemakers
			Discerning of spirits		Oratory
	Helps			Ruling	
	Governments			Showing mercy	
	Diversities of tongues	Tongues interpretation	Kinds of tongues Interpretation of tongues		

follow a certain order. When a difference does occur, it is minor. For example, should giving be above healing or below discerning of spirits? The Scripture is not clear so I have put it at the halfway point. Move it up or down as you may desire, but it should not go above exhortation nor should it go below ruling and governments.

It is, in fact, of minor importance to note in detail the position of each gift. What is important to see is that there is a general sequence every time the gifts of the Spirit are listed. And I have put wisdom, knowledge and faith in the slot with apostles, prophets and evangelists. They certainly do not correspond to these three, but it is inconceivable that apostles, prophets and evangelists could get along without the gifts of wisdom, knowledge and faith. However, a person might have these latter three gifts without being either an apostle, prophet or evangelist. They do fall into the upper structure at a high level, however.

When we are exhorted to seek the best gifts, this chart can serve as a guide to give us some clues as to what we should be seeking. But remember, what may be the best gift in the list, may not be the best gift for you. After all, if all were evangelists like myself, the Body of Christ, the Church, would consist of little more than one great big tongue trying to say many different things at the same time. It takes every gift in the Church to make the Church a complete and proper body.

The addendum is added but separated from the rest of the chart. It is meant only for informative consideration. There is no way of knowing how the items in that column would fit into the chart. And in my estimation some would not fit into the chart at all. They would simply stand as part of God's Word, but certainly not as special gifts from the Holy Spirit.

What is best needed, however, is not a grasping for gifts but to have a heart attitude that is aptly prayed in this hymn:

O Comforter, gentle and tender,
    O holy and heavenly Dove,
We are yielding our hearts in surrender,
    We're waiting Thy fullness to prove.

Oh come as the heart searching fire,
    Oh come as the sin-cleansing flood;
Consume us with holy desire
    And fill with the fullness of God.

Anoint us with gladness and healing;
    Baptize us with power from on high;
Oh come with Thy filling and sealing
    While low at Thy footstool we lie.

—Albert B. Simpson

Chapter 5

The Grieving Spirit

One might think that in a book such as this there would be a chapter proving specifically that the Holy Spirit is a person. This I have not thought necessary, having already shown in chapter one that the Holy Spirit is God. So a person He is indeed.

Being a person, the Holy Spirit can be insulted. Hebrews 10:29 tells us, "How much more severely do you think a man deserves to be punished who has trampled the Son of God under foot, who has treated as an unholy thing the blood of the covenant that sanctified him, and who has insulted the Spirit of grace?"

Being a person, the Holy Spirit can be provoked. Psalm 78:40 says, "How they rebelled against him in the desert and grieved him in the wasteland!" Later on in this chapter we will be shown that the "him" referred to here is the Holy Spirit of God.

Being a person, the Holy Spirit can be blasphemed. "And so I tell you, every sin and blasphemy will be forgiven men, but the blasphemy against the Spirit will not be forgiven" (Matthew 12:31). This is one reason I say the Holy Spirit is the most tenderhearted Person of the Trinity.

This Scripture verse and the ones following in Matthew indicate that God will forgive just about anything and everything that man can do to Him. But when we deliberately attribute to the devil or Satan what the Holy Spirit has done, this is blasphemy of a nature that is never forgiven.

(Note: It is a good Christian policy to give the devil credit for absolutely nothing. He rejoices in praise, attention and any kind of recognition. I do not even spell his names with capitals as you may have just noticed.)

Being a person, the Holy Spirit can be grieved. In fact, being so tenderhearted, the Holy Spirit is very easily grieved. I want you to see how easily He is grieved, even though we are warned not to grieve Him, "And do not grieve the Holy Spirit of God, with whom you were sealed for the day of redemption" (Ephesians 4:30) is a direct command. In this we must not be mistaken.

The Church must understand that the Holy Spirit is easily grieved. But it appears the Church has failed to realize that truth. Many churches do not see the full blessing of God upon them because they are grieving the Holy Spirit in various ways.

For example, many churches seem content to remain small bodies of believers with little or no outreach to the lost who surround them. These congregations are often called "struggling little works." However, it is generally not the church that is struggling. It is the pastor who is struggling. He struggles with the elected board to get freedom to enact a program that will be able to reach the masses. He struggles with the congregation, urging the people to meet God so the Holy Spirit can work.

He also struggles with his finances. He has pledged himself before God and man to do the work of the ministry. But the congregation does not grow to give him more material support. The budget committee callously gives him a salary on which not one of them would venture to live. Any suggestion that the nine men on his board might put their salaries into a pot each week, divide it into ten equal portions, and give one-tenth to the pastor for an average wage and living, only succeeds in bringing cries of horror and outrage.

But even that would not be enough to satisfy the biblical pattern. The Bible says, "The elders who direct the affairs of the church well are worthy of double honor, especially those whose work is preaching and teaching. For the Scripture says, 'Do not muzzle the ox while it is treading out the grain,' and 'The worker deserves his wages' " (1 Timothy 5:17-18). Comparing this with a parallel passage, Paul says, "Yes, this was written for us. . . . If we have sown spiritual seed among you, is it too much if we reap a material harvest from you?" (1 Corinthians 9:10-11).

Put it all together. The pastor is to receive a double salary, not half a salary as is so often the case. "If God can keep him humble, we can keep him poor" is a joke that I do not consider funny at all. It is a terrible grievance to the Holy Spirit who has given different orders. The pastor is to humble himself. The congregation is to see that he is abundantly supplied with material goods.

No, there is no indication in the Scriptures that the man of God is to struggle with his finances. Nor do the Scriptures indicate that he is to provide his own living. Oh, yes. Paul did it by making tents. But listen to what he says to the Corinthians when they would not take care of him properly: "Don't you know that those who work in the temple get their food from the temple, and those who serve at the altar in what is offered on the altar? In the same way, the Lord has commanded that those who preach the gospel should receive their living from the gospel" (1 Corinthians 9:13-14). Then because they would not look after him financially, he rebukes them with, "I robbed other churches by receiving support from them so as to serve you" (2 Corinthians 11:8).

Note here that he did not earn all his living in Corinth by making tents. Other churches assisted him by their missionary outreach. And by the way, why do so many people and churches want to be like the Corinthian church by being so stingy with their pastors? Surely if the Bible were being written now instead of then, we would not want our church to be labeled as the most carnal in all history—and maybe even get our names printed in the epistle for outstanding rebellion and stubbornness.

"But," you might say, "I did not know these things."

Well, that is the point of this whole chapter. The Holy Spirit is so tenderhearted that He can be grieved just by our not knowing—by our ignorance. And He tells us that we are not to be ignorant. I want us all to grasp this. It will get us into the Word of God again. It will give us a real desire to know His mind and will.

Psalm 78 is a long psalm with seventy-two verses, and, like other Psalms, it was written to be sung. Imagine listening to the rabbi in the synagogue on a Sabbath morning as he brings the worship time to a close: "We will close our worship with the singing of Psalm 78. Since we have gone a little past the hour today, to save some time, we will omit verse three." By doing so in a service we actually save about one-fifty millionth of a person's allotted time here on earth.

How conscious we are of time, especially the closing time rather than the opening time. We have become so time conscious the Holy Spirit is grieved. We are told that a sermon should be a half hour or less in order to be of value. Where do we get this? Certainly it is not shown in the Scriptures, nor has the philosophy proven its worth in practice.

In Acts 20:7-12 we see exactly the opposite as Paul is meeting with Christians at Troas for a fellowship supper. He spoke until midnight. That could have been five hours or more. Then at midnight they had a little recess to restore the dead to life, and he continued speaking to them until sunrise. I know that this is an extreme case, but so are half-hour sermons if we take any direction from the Word of God. I have yet to see a Holy Spirit revival where long, Bible-saturated preaching has not preceded the revival itself, or been a part of the revival.

Now back to Psalm 78. Verse 40, almost the very heart of the Psalm, says, "How often they rebelled against him in the desert and grieved him in the wasteland!" The Holy Spirit was being grieved during forty years of wilderness wanderings.

The Israelites refused to allow Moses to lead them directly into the Promised Land. They could only see the obstacles and would not trust God for victory over the giants in the land. I suppose they wanted God to clear out the giants first, then they would venture forth. God had dried up the Red Sea without their action, so they went by sight. Next they were to learn to go by faith, but they would not. They refused to obey the commands of God through Moses.

Yes, they grieved the Holy Spirit. "But you have not shown that the 'Him' in the verse is the Holy Spirit," you say, "and the verse does not say everything you are making it say."

Psalm 95:7-11 gives more detail. Obviously the verses speak of the same situation in the wilderness wanderings. "Today, if you hear his voice, do not harden your hearts as you did at Meribah, as you did that day at Massah in the desert, where your fathers tested and tried me, though they had seen what I did. For forty years I was angry with that generation; I said, 'They are a people whose hearts go astray, and they have not known my ways.' So I declared on oath in my anger, 'They shall never enter my rest.' "

God's people had seen what He was able to do. But they hardened their hearts against their God. They saw the Red Sea open up so they could go through unimpeded. Then they watched as the waters closed in upon the Egyptians. They even sang a song Moses wrote about it, as it is recorded in Exodus 15:1-18.

Further in Exodus 15 they saw God turn the undrinkable, bitter water into drinkable, sweet water. In chapter 16 He provided meat by sending quail flying into their camps about three feet off the ground. This He did each evening (compare Numbers 11:31), and in the morning they received manna just for the picking up.

In Exodus 17 they saw God produce water from a rock in an area where there is no water. And many other such miracles occurred. But instead of continually praising the Lord and seeking to understand all this, they did not learn from the lessons. They grumbled instead. Now the Spirit was grieved with their grumbling as well, but Psalm 95:7-11 teaches only that He was grieved because they did not know His ways.

David, writing in the psalm quoted above, says that in spite of all these things God did, the Israelites erred in their hearts and failed to understand what God was really doing for them. They saw what He did, but did not understand His ways.

Still the psalmist does not pinpoint "Him" as being the Holy Spirit. As we read, reread and read the Bible again and again, however, certain hidden truths begin to emerge. The Bible is its own best interpreter. Tying the New Testament into verses I have used in Psalms 78 and 95, shows very plainly that the Holy Spirit is indicated, and not the Father or the Son. From Hebrews 3:7-11 (emphasis added) we read:

> So as the Holy Spirit says:
> "Today, if you hear his voice,
>   do not harden your hearts
> as you did in the rebellion,
>   during the time of testing in the desert,
> where your fathers tested and tried *me*
>   and for forty years saw what *I* did.
> That is why *I* was angry with that
>   generation,
>   and *I* said, 'Their hearts are always going
>   astray,
>   and they have not known *my* ways.'
> So I declared on oath in *my* anger,
>   'They shall never enter *my* rest.' "

Notice that this is a complete repetition of Psalm 95:7-11, except for the beginning of verse 7 in Hebrews. And in verse 7 who is the designated speaker? None other than the Holy Spirit. "So as the Holy Spirit says: . . ."

So the Holy Spirit is the Person of the Godhead who was grieved. He was grieved simply because the people remained ignorant of who He was, what He wanted done and how He wanted to do it.

Grieve in these passages means to wound the feelings of another person. It is a personal sorrow. "And do not grieve the Holy Spirit of God . . ." (Ephesians 4:30). We are not to wound the Holy Spirit's feelings and bring Him personal sorrow. To avoid this we must get back into God's Word and the place of prayer.

That we all grieve Him there can be little doubt since we can simply grieve Him by our ignorance. But let us pledge ourselves to gaining a deeper understanding of Him—get into the Word He has spoken and seek His ways.

Now this is just the ground level. It is the bottom rung on the ladder. I want us to see that if we can grieve Him simply by our ignorance, everything else beyond this certainly must grieve Him even more. How careful we ought to be in our actions and words.

The children of Israel did not know the Holy Spirit's ways. But they did not have to remain at that level. The psalmist David prayed seven times in the Psalms to have God's ways revealed to him. Then he mentions these ways more than fifty other times in his writings. And look at Moses. He knew God's ways as seen in Psalm 103:7. Yes, he knew the ways of the Holy Spirit.

So can we. Let us discover His ways and cease grieving Him. We can begin by praying:

> Breathe on me, Breath of God,
> 　Fill me with life anew,
> That I may love what Thou dost love,
> 　And do what Thou wouldst do.

> Breathe on me, Breath of God,
> 　Until my heart is pure,
> Until with Thee I will one will
> 　To do or to endure.

> Breathe on me, Breath of God,
> 　Till I am wholly Thine,
> Till all this earthly part of me
> 　Glows with Thy fire divine.

> Breathe on me, Breath of God,
> 　So shall I never die,
> But live with Thee the perfect life
> 　Of Thine eternity.

> —Edwin Hatch

Chapter 6

Resisting the Spirit

Grieving the Spirit is a serious matter. We have seen how easy it is to grieve Him—just by being ignorant of His ways. Could we conclude, therefore, that in more evident and crucial matters He is very deeply grieved? In this chapter we will progress to a deeper grieving.

Being a person, the Holy Spirit can be resisted. We need to understand many more things about grieving to get the import of resisting. All of our contrary acts toward the Holy Spirit cause His feelings to be wounded. He grieves because of our ignorance. How much more He must grieve when we deliberately do things that are contrary to the Word.

When we begin to grow in the Christian walk we are bound to find out some of the many things that grieve Him. Then, knowing what God wants of us, if we deliberately refuse to heed His command, "Touch no unclean thing," (2 Corinthians 6:17), something deeper than a superficial grieving takes place. When He speaks to us about certain things and we fail to respond positively, then He is resisted.

This resisting does not necessarily mean refusing to give up an evil habit. It can also come when He speaks to us about some type of service to the Lord and to others. When our old nature says "no" to this, then we are resisting in another form.

I have been asked on a number of occasions, "But you do not expect visible results every time you preach, do you?" Putting the question in the negative helps a person to respond negatively. But my answer is always positive. I surely do expect visible results every time I preach.

We should all expect God to work through us at all times. However, sometimes the results are not all that we may have anticipated. Until chapter 7 in Acts, nearly everything worked out so gloriously: ". . . three thousand were added. . . . The Lord added to their number daily. . . . The number of men grew to about five thousand. . . . More and more men and women believed. . . . The number of disciples increased rapidly" (Acts 2:41, 47; 4:4; 5:14; 6:7).

Then after all these results from both public ser-vices and private witnessing, something seemed to go wrong. Stephen preaches a sermon that appears to far outshine Peter's in structure and content. And the audience stones him to death (Acts 7:59-60).

Near the end of his recorded message he gives us a verse that strikes home in this study, "You stiff-necked people, with uncircumcised hearts and ears! You are just like your fathers: You always resist the Holy Spirit!" (Acts 7:51).

Resisting means to hinder, stand against or oppose. Thousands were turning to the Lord in those days. However, there were still those who stood against the working of the Holy Spirit as He spoke to them. They not only rejected His wooings to bring them to Jesus Christ as Savior and Lord, they also opposed the workers of the gospel through whom the Holy Spirit was working. Thus they were hindering Him, and, more than that, they were standing against Him.

You might say that Stephen's message was pretty scathing and that he got carried away a little emotionally. But not so. We read, "But Stephen, full of the Holy Spirit . . ." (Acts 7:55). Being full of the Holy Spirit means to have the fruit of the Spirit. One of the flavors is gentleness. Another is meekness. Another is self-control.

The fault lies with the listeners, not Stephen. They were resisting the Holy Spirit. That included Saul of Tarsus who was later converted and became the great Apostle Paul. It really was quite a meeting. In it were "the elders and the teachers of the law. They seized Stephen and brought him before the Sanhedrin" (Acts 6:12). Stephen reached for the top and got top resistance. Since Stephen was full of the Holy Spirit, the Holy Spirit was certainly being resisted.

To whom was Stephen referring when he mentions their fathers resisting the Holy Spirit? We do not know particularly, but there are many Old

Testament situations that fit. One is found very early in the Bible: "Then the LORD said, 'My Spirit will not contend with man forever, for he is mortal; his days will be a hundred and twenty years'" (Genesis 6:3).

Here was striving against the Holy Spirit. Striving against is resisting. People all over the world, as it was known before the flood, were resisting the Holy Spirit.

There was Noah of whom it is written, ". . . he walked with God" (Genesis 6:9). In Hebrews 11:7 we find that Noah feared God, preached to the world and gave them the biggest object lesson ever given by using the ark, and was himself saved by faith. "By faith Noah, when warned about things not yet seen, in holy fear built an ark to save his family. By his faith he condemned the world and became heir of the righteousness that comes by faith." He is also called "a preacher of righteousness" (2 Peter 2:5).

Through Noah, the Holy Spirit convicted people of sin, righteousness and judgment. And God waited for a response with long-suffering (1 Peter 3:20). But there was no response except from Noah's immediate family. There was this extreme lack of response because the masses chose to resist the Holy Spirit.

Resisting is not like grieving the Holy Spirit by ignorance. Resisting is a deliberate act of the will. These people were actually striving against the Holy Spirit in a personal battle.

Noah and his immediate family were not the only

ones preaching. According to the chronologies, there were others preaching almost right up to the time of the flood. This assertion may get us into difficulty with some Bible scholars. The modern student says that the chronologies are not reliable, speaking from one side of his mouth. From the other side of his mouth he says that he believes in the plenary verbal inerrancy of the Bible as originally given. There is something wrong with this kind of thinking.

For this study we will accept the Bible just as it is and take just what it says. Whether the "begots" refer to sons, grandsons, or great-grandsons does not alter the figures in the following chart. The chart is not original. I saw it first many years ago when the late George M. Blackett, cofounder and first president of Canadian Bible College, Regina, used it in a study in Genesis.

A CHRONOLOGICAL CHART				
Seth's Line	Date of birth	Age at birth of son	Age at death	Date of death
Adam	0	130	930	930
Seth	130	105	912	1042
Enos	235	90	905	1140
Cainan	325	70	910	1235
Mahalalel	395	65	895	1290
Jared	460	162	962	1422
Enoch	622	65	365	987
Methuselah	687	187	969	1656*
Lamech	874	182	777	1651
Noah	1056	502	950	2006
*The flood would be in 1656 A.M. (Anno Mundi—in the year of the world)				

According to the chart, Enoch died less than 700 years before the flood. And remember what is said of Enoch: "Enoch walked with God . . ." (Genesis 5:22), ". . . For before he was taken, he was commended as one who pleased God" (Hebrews 11:5). He is also called a prophet: "And Enoch also, the seventh from Adam prophesied of these . . ." (Jude 14,KJV). The older people who died in the flood would have heard of Enoch and some would have even heard him preach. But they resisted his message. So they are among the "fathers" who resisted the Holy Spirit, as referred to in Stephen's sermon.

Enoch had a son named Methuselah, born when Enoch was sixty-five years old. Methuselah would have heard his father preach for 300 years, most of the time with understanding.

It is interesting to note that since Adam lived to be 930 years old, Adam lived for 243 years after Methuselah was born. In other words, Methuselah could have received the story of the Garden of Eden, the Fall and the results of the Fall firsthand from Adam. Those who resisted the Holy Spirit until their deaths in the flood could have had accurate information of God's dealings with man if they had listened to Methuselah.

It appears Enoch named his son prophetically. Besides "man of the javelin," the name Methuselah means "he dies," and "the sending forth." This would indicate that he was the strong, athletic type at whose death the floods would be sent forth. A running paraphrase of the meaning of his name would then be: When he dies the floods will begin. According to Jewish tradition, Methuselah died seven days before the flood. This is based on Genesis 7:10: "And after the seven days the flood-waters came on the earth."

As his prophetic name indicates, Methuselah would be a preacher of righteousness, preaching that death comes to all even though they lived so very long, and that God would destroy the earth with a flood. But they resisted his message. They resisted the Holy Spirit.

Lamech, Methuselah's son, was also a preacher of righteousness. This is indicated when Lamech named his son. He named him Noah because, "He will comfort us in the labor and painful toil of our hands caused by the ground the LORD has cursed" (Genesis 5:29). He too, would know all about this curse firsthand. Adam lived until Lamech was twenty-eight. And Lamech lived until five years before the flood. The people resisted his message. They resisted the Holy Spirit.

What a terrible resisting there was. What a terrible judgment followed. The people strove against the Holy Spirit. They fought against God.

Many of us have heard Christians say, "If I only had my life to live over again!" Perhaps God had spoken to them about some type of vocation. But they would not listen. Or they listened but would not obey. Or they obeyed at first, but lacked the discipline to carry through.

I think of a sixteen-year-old girl who had responded to a call for missionary recruitment.

Shortly afterward, in conversation, she told me the Lord had given her a job and went on to describe her newfound employment.

"But how can you keep up with your school work doing a job like that?" I exclaimed questioningly.

"Oh, I have quit school." She looked delighted.

"But how are you ever going to fulfill your desire to be a foreign missionary if you do not finish high school so you can go to Bible college?" I inquired.

"Oh, I am going to do it my way," came the response.

I counseled her that it would not work. She needed to follow the proven pattern. People do not get to be foreign missionaries who drop out of school when they are in grade ten. She brushed my advice aside.

We moved away from that pastorate in a couple of years. Some years after that my wife received a letter from this lady. She wanted to come and live with us to get reestablished. She had married an unsaved man and had three children. He beat her and the children mercilessly and ran around with another woman.

I do not know the end of the story. But this Christian lady resisted the preaching and instruction of righteousness. She resisted the Holy Spirit. She said, "I will have my way." And God let her.

We can grieve the Holy Spirit simply by our ignorance. In this He shows great patience with us.

But when we grieve Him deliberately, we are resisting Him. For this, many times judgment falls and we are the losers. Let us not resist Him. Let us deliberately pray instead:

> Search me, Oh God, my actions try,
>   And let my life appear
> As seen by Thine all-searching eye—
>   To mine, my ways make clear.
>
> Search all my thoughts, the secret springs,
>   The motives that control,
> The chambers where polluted things
>   Hold empire o'er my soul.
>
> Search, till Thy fiery glance has cast
>   Its holy light through all,
> And I by grace am brought at last
>   Before Thy face to fall.
>
> Thus, prostrate I shall learn of Thee
>   What now I feebly prove—
> That God alone in Christ can be
>   Unutterable love.
>
> —Frank Bottome

Chapter 7

Quenching the Spirit

We cannot unconsciously grieve the Holy Spirit for long without beginning to resist Him. Somewhere along the way we learn right from wrong. Then what was an unconscious grieving, becomes conscious, willful grieving. This is resisting.

If we continue to resist Him, something else begins to happen in our lives. This is true whether we are children of God or children of this world. There comes a time when the Holy Spirit seems to say that it is enough. This is called quenching the Spirit.

There is a delightful little book in the Bible called First Thessalonians. It is a simple epistle of Paul to the church at Thessalonica, Greece, right at the northern extremity of the Aegean Sea. It is very likely the first epistle that Paul wrote. Therefore it is somewhat simpler than most of the others.

There is no rebuke or correction given in this epistle. It is just a friendly little letter of commendation and teaching. In the last chapter Paul uses some very short sentences. This is very unlike some of his later epistles, where one sentence may last for a number of verses. These very long sentences become difficult to understand. But there is no mistaking the meaning of the short one we will look at in this chapter.

Paul says: "Be joyful always; pray continually; give thanks in all cicumstances. . . . Do not put out [quench, KJV] the Spirit's fire; do not treat prophecies with contempt. Test everything. Hold on to the good. Avoid every kind of evil" (1 Thessalonians 5:16-22).

Right in the middle of these short sentences is the injunction, "Do not put out [quench, KJV] the Spirit's fire" (5:19). *Quench* here means to put out, like a fire. In other words, do not put the fire of the Holy Spirit out of your lives.

This is a notable injunction. It is a command. It is almost as though the Thessalonians had been doing something wrong, and Paul orders them to stop. However, no wrong act is mentioned in the epistle. All through the epistle Paul appears to be giving only friendly advice. So we must look for something else, some other reason for the verse.

The most dramatic type of the Holy Spirit in the Bible is fire. Further, very little is ever mentioned about the fire of Pentecost, even though one of the manifestations on the Day of Pentecost was a tongue of fire that sat on each person individually. This is quite overlooked when we hear of the experience of Pentecost being repeated in people's lives today.

I do not say that the tongue of fire is necessary to be filled with the Holy Spirit. What I am saying is that we should not call something that which it is not. If the total manifestation is not there, why call it the Pentecostal experience?

In order to call an experience the Pentecostal experience, a group of people would have to hear the mighty rushing wind. They would have to have a tongue of fire on each person in the group. And they would have to have every person speaking in a language that foreigners would be able to understand as the gospel was being given in this manner.

In all my evangelistic travels over the entire continent, and with pastoral experience in five Canadian provinces besides, I have yet to see or even hear of all these three things happening in any church or assembly at the same time. It stands alone as it is recorded in Acts chapter 2 on the Day of Pentecost being celebrated in Jerusalem about A.D. 29.

These three things are, however, alluded to in Acts 11:15 where Peter says, "As I began to speak, the Holy Spirit came on them as he had come on us at the beginning." If this includes the wind, fire and tongues, then it should not be used as a proof text for tongues alone. And tongues is the manifestation that is generally lifted from this text.

It is interesting to notice Peter's terminology, ". . . as he had come on us at the beginning." A considerable period of time has elapsed between Acts chapter 2 and Acts chapter 11. There have been four periods of persecution between the two chapters. It is generally considered that about eight years have passed between Pentecost and the time that Peter is reporting this verse to the Council at Jerusalem.

Now Peter is relating to this Council that the phenomenon has happened again, a second time. It had not been happening all the time, or he would not have said, "at the beginning." He would have used a term such as "as usual." Notice too, that he tells them that it was like it happened to "us." This was the select few, 120 of which the Council was a part.

In Acts 19:6 we read, "When Paul placed his hands on them, the Holy Spirit came on them, and they spoke in tongues and prophesied." I have never heard anybody call this the Ephesus experience. It might well be called "the ordinary experience" since it took place on just an ordinary day, quite unlike the very special day called the Feast of Pentecost.

It cannot be the equivalent of Pentecost which featured the first outpouring, since at the outpouring at Ephesus there was the laying on of hands. And at Ephesus only tongues is mentioned, without the tongues of fire and the mighty rushing wind, while prophecy is added.

We see fire used as a symbol of God's power in many other places throughout the Scriptures. I will pick out a few representative ones, beginning in Genesis.

When God expelled Adam and Eve from the Garden of Eden, "After he drove the man out, he placed on the east side of the Garden of Eden cherubim and a flaming sword flashing back and forth to guard the way to the tree of life" (Genesis 3:24).

God appeared to Moses in the fiery bush when Moses was in the backside of the desert getting his thinking straightened out; "There the angel of the LORD appeared to him in flames of fire from within a bush. Moses saw that though the bush was on fire it did not burn up" (Exodus 3:2).

Ten chapters later we read, "By day the LORD went ahead of them in a pillar of cloud to guide them on their way and by night in a pillar of fire to give them light, so that they could travel by day or night. Neither the pillar of cloud by day nor the pillar of fire by night left its place in front of the people" (Exodus 13:21-22).

When Nadab and Abihu "offered unauthorized fire before the LORD. . . . So fire came out from the presence of the LORD and consumed them . . ." (Leviticus 10:1-2).

When Elijah contended with the prophets of Baal, God answered by fire. "Then the fire of the LORD fell and burned up the sacrifice, the wood, the stones and the soil, and also licked up the water in the trench. . . . They fell prostrate and cried, 'The LORD—he is God! The LORD—he is God!' " (1 Kings 18:38-39).

The psalmist David said, "'I will watch my ways and keep my tongue from sin; I will put a muzzle on

my mouth as long as the wicked are in my presence.
. . .' As I meditated, the fire burned; then I spoke
with my tongue" (Psalm 39:1-3).

Isaiah wrote, "Then one of the seraphs flew to
me with a live coal in his hand, which he had
taken with tongs from the altar. With it he
touched my mouth and said, 'See, this has
touched your lips; your guilt is taken away and
your sin atoned for' " (Isaiah 6:6-7).

When John the Baptist was preaching and baptizing at the Jordan River, he said, "I baptize you with
water for repentance. But after me will come one
who is more powerful than I, whose sandals I am
not fit to carry. He will baptize you with the Holy
Spirit and with fire. His winnowing fork is in his
hand, and he will clear his threshing floor, gathering
the wheat into the barn and burning up the chaff
with unquenchable fire" (Matthew 3:11-12).

To summarize the above, the Holy Spirit gives
direction and protection, speaks messages, proves
Himself to the sinners, shows His power, heats
cold hearts, fires men's mouths to witness and
burns the impurities from Christians' hearts.

When we continue to resist Him in all these
things, the time comes when He is quenched. No
definite time period is indicated. The Holy Spirit
is very gracious in His long-suffering. But the
time does come when He decides that it is
enough. He decides to stop wooing the sinner. He
decides to stop convicting the saint. He determines that it is a waste of time. The individual has
made up his mind to reject the working of the

Holy Spirit. So He is quenched. The fire has been put out.

How many people I have met who have once walked in the way of grace, even having served the Lord in a full-time spiritual ministry. But now they are calloused and indifferent. They not only seem unconcerned for themselves, but they are also unconcerned about the fate of their children. I can think of nothing more terrible than bringing a child into the world and then seeing that descendant go out into a Christless eternity. It ought to be the most terrifying experience ever, to bear a child, see him mature physically and mentally, and then allow him to go into the fires of hell as an unregenerated sinner. But it happens.

I have a front page picture and story in my files from one of the nation's leading newspapers. It is the unusual testimony of a businessman who had walked with God and who had been miraculously healed from blindness.

But later in life he got far from God. He even took an oath in his own blood in a secret order, claiming that his blood oath was stronger than the blood of Christ. I counseled him that "the blood of Jesus, his Son, purifies us from all sin" (1 John 1:7), and that he must return to the Lord. But he could not or would not see that the work of Christ on the cross was sufficient for any need. His own blood oath was sufficient according to him. His blindness was worse now than before, for his present spiritual blindness far exceeded his former physical blindness.

A child of God had resisted the Holy Spirit until the Holy Spirit was quenched. He had put out the Holy Spirit.

Shortly after my own salvation in the summer of 1948, my home church began to experience a moving of the Holy Spirit under the ministry of evangelist Jimmy Mercer. For these special meetings, Jimmy insisted that there be a forty-voice choir. The Hayward brothers put me between them in the choir and tried to teach me to sing bass. I did not learn to sing too well, but I learned a lot by watching the crowd as Jimmy preached.

Every night for a number of weeks, a huge man attended the services with his wife. Every night as the choir sang the invitation hymn he stood unconcerned, looking around, even sneering. Every night his wife stood with him with head bowed, praying, and sometimes weeping. On occasions she spoke to him as we sang, obviously asking him to go forward.

One night the evangelist did something I have never done, nor do I intend to do it. He left the pulpit as we sang, walked down the aisle and stopped right beside the giant of a man.

He reached up, took hold of the lapels of the man's coat and said, "Why don't you get saved?"

I shall never forget the answer. It boomed out over the hushed crowd and the singing of the choir. The English was poor. The answer was terrifying, especially to one so new to the faith such as I. He said, "God don't speak to me anymore!"

A child of the devil had resisted the Holy Spirit until the Holy Spirit was quenched. He had put out the Holy Spirit. The Holy Spirit no longer spoke to him.

Thirty years later I questioned two of the elders in the church about this individual. Neither knew his whereabouts. Neither knew what had happened to him. Neither knew if he were dead or alive. And all of us agreed that whereas once we all prayed for him to be saved, somewhere along the line he had been lost in the multitude of our activities and thoughts.

How careful we need to be. The Holy Spirit is so easily grieved, but even when we grieve Him He still woos us. But when we resist Him too long, He is quenched. He is put out. Let us not put out the fire of God. Let us rather pray:

> O fire of God, begin in me;
>   Burn out the dross of self and sin,
> Burn off my fetters, set me free,
>   And make my heart a heaven within.
>
> Baptize with fire this soul of mine;
>   Endue me with Thy Spirit's might
> And make me by Thy power divine
>   A burning and a shining light.
>
> Burn in, O fire of God, burn in
>   Till all my soul Christ's image bears,
> And every power and pulse within
>   His holy, heavenly nature wears.

Burn on, O fire of God, burn on
   Till all my dross is burned away,
Till earth and sin and self are gone,
   And I can stand the testing day.

—Albert B. Simpson

Chapter 8

Vexing the Spirit

A question may have troubled you as you read the last chapter. If not, I will raise the issue myself: What about the prayers of that godly wife whose husband said, "God don't speak to me anymore"? What about my own prayers on behalf of the man who had been healed from blindness? Does God not answer prayer?

Yes. God does answer prayer. He is faithful to His promise: "Believe in the Lord Jesus, and you will be saved—you and your household" (Acts 16:31). God delights in household salvation, and Jesus said, "Again, I tell you that if two of you on earth agree about anything you ask for, it will be done for you by my Father in heaven" (Matthew 18:19).

Yes, God does answer prayer. And some of His ways of doing so are very special ways. Some of them are hard for us to understand even as Paul noted: "Oh, the depth of the riches of the wisdom and knowledge of God! How unsearchable his judgments, and his paths beyond tracing out!" (Romans 11:33).

Isaiah gives us a little but important key to one of God's methods. It is not easily understood. But the fact of it is there: "Yet they rebelled and grieved his Holy Spirit. So he turned and became their enemy and he himself fought against them" (Isaiah 63:10).

The children of Israel had rebelled against the LORD. They rebelled at Sinai and set up a golden calf to worship. They rebelled at Shittim and took the unsaved daughters of Moab to be their wives. They rebelled in the Promised Land and insisted on having a king. The list could go on and on.

They grieved the Holy Spirit until they were openly resisting Him. They resisted the Holy Spirit until He was quenched or put out. But did this nullify God's covenant promise to Israel? That promise was like His prayer promises to us today. No. God will keep His Word.

Paul in writing to the young pastor Titus said, "God, who does not lie . . ." (Titus 1:2). This he quoted from Numbers 23:19 which reads, "God is not a man, that he should lie, nor a son of man, that he should change his mind. Does he speak and then not act? Does he promise and not fulfill?"

So even when the Holy Spirit is quenched, He will begin to respond to our prayers and to His own promises and covenants. When He is quenched for so long, He becomes vexed. Yes. We can vex Him. This is a very sore grieving. When He is vexed, He begins to fight against us.

This is not a vengeful fighting. It is not a punitive fighting. It is not a fighting to prove a point. It is not even a fighting to regain respect. It is a fighting to gain our attention in order that we might be brought to our senses.

You may have prayed or heard somebody else pray, "Oh, God! Do anything! Just save my son!" Or for yourself, "Oh, God. Make me willing!" Or, "Do anything to me, Lord. I just want to get rid of this dirty habit."

How can God answer this type of praying? In order to do so, He must take drastic action at times. And when the Holy Spirit is vexed He does take drastic action. He does not eliminate our wills. But there are occasions when He brings along certain circumstances to make us willing.

God answered Stephen's prayer that is recorded in Acts 7:60, "Lord, do not hold this sin against them. . . ." Later on, in order to get the attention of Saul of Tarsus, God struck him down to the ground with blindness (Acts 9). He had been among those that resisted the Holy Spirit during Stephen's sermon: "And Saul was there, giving approval to his death" (Acts 8:1).

Against Israel's rebellion, He turned on them in His vexation: "Without pity the Lord has swallowed up all the dwellings of Jacob; . . . In fierce anger he has cut off every horn of Israel. . . . He has burned in Jacob like a flaming fire that consumes everything around it. Like an enemy he has strung his bow; his right hand is ready. Like a foe he has slain all who were pleasing to the eye; he has poured out his wrath like fire . . ." (Lamentations 2:2-5).

In the thirty-six places where *vexed* is used in Holy Writ it is always with the idea of battle, fighting or oppression. When we vex the Holy Spirit, He battles us to the place where He can talk to us, where we will listen, and where we will respond.

It is a terrible thing to vex the Holy Spirit, as we can see from the above. And it happens today.

I was in a series of meetings that eventually went for a full seven weeks. During this time the cooperating pastors and I usually met for prayer in the early afternoon. One afternoon one of the pastors requested prayer for his wayward son who was far from God. I replied that we would indeed pray. I also decided to talk to this pastor about his son, since I would be having the evening meal with him.

"Where is your son during the services?" I inquired.

"I don't know. He is away with the car," came the response.

"Whose car is it?" I got personal.

"It is my car," came the logical answer.

"Who pays for the gas when he uses your car during the services?" I continued.

"I guess you would say that I do." The hesitant reply came as though he knew the direction in which I was heading.

"You know your son smokes. Do you also know that he smokes more than just ordinary tobacco?" I had to convince him that I had enough experience to know. "Who pays for all this?" I went on.

"We give him an allowance."

"It takes a pretty hefty allowance to take care of a drug habit," I commented, thinking he would realize that his son might be getting the money in another way.

"We give him a very large allowance," he replied.

Finally I said to him as kindly as possible, "We have been praying for your son for a number of weeks now. Others may have been for much longer. Hear me out. You give him a free room. You feed him and clothe him. Then you give him your car with free gas, and enough money to support his sinful, evil habit."

The lad was not home for supper, having taken off right after school. So I continued, "When he comes home tonight I want you to have some ground rules written out. Do them in duplicate so you can give him a copy and have one for yourself for future reference.

"The ground rules should include that as long as he lives in your home and puts his feet under your table, he will have to obey all these rules. Further, you will work out an agreement whereby the car is used only for purposes that become the church of Jesus Christ."

There was more to follow, but I was interrupted by, "But if I do all this, I will lose my boy!"

"That is quite impossible," I voiced my opinion. "You have already lost him. And now he uses you and the Lord for a tool."

He quietly said, "I see what you mean."

But my advice was too late. Very late that Thursday night after we had prayed with many people at the altar, I was preparing to retire. I received a phone call. I was to go to the hospital immediately to pray for a young man who was in intensive care due to a very serious car accident. It was my friend's car. It was my friend's son.

The nurse told me that I could have only five minutes, although she was very gracious about it. As I entered the intensive care unit, I announced who I was, telling the lad that someone had called me to pray for him.

He responded very feebly. His limbs were in traction. His head was bandaged. His eyes were nearly swollen shut. "I asked you to come," he said. "But I know you won't pray for me if I am going to continue living for the devil. Please forgive me for not attending the services. I am coming back to God."

I forgave him and told him that his father was just outside the door with another minister. "I only asked for you," he replied, "but maybe I need to speak to my dad before you pray."

I opened the doors and beckoned for them to come in. As he was asking forgiveness from his father, I was preparing to anoint him with oil and pray for him according to James 5:14-15: "Is any one of you sick? He should call the elders of the church to pray over him and anoint him with oil in the name of the Lord. And the prayer offered in faith will make the sick person well; the Lord will raise him up. If he has sinned, he will be forgiven."

As we were praying the nurse came in, perhaps to see why there were three men beside the bed instead of one. If that were the case, she immediately forgot her mission. As soon as we were through praying she exclaimed, "What have you got in that bottle! Just look at what has happened to him!"

There he was. His eyes had cleared, not only from the shock of the accident but also from the drugs. He endeavored to sit up, but his restrainers prevented him.

By now it was nearly Friday morning. Another event had taken place that we were not aware of earlier Thursday night. The crusade treasurer had arrived home just before midnight. He had been trying to locate me ever since. He finally did so at the hospital. Somebody had had a pot party in his bedroom while the crusade was in progress. The intruders had taken all the offerings covering a period of about four weeks. We had special prayer that the thieves would be convicted of their sin and come to know Christ. It was no big deal. I only needed sufficient money to keep my body and soul together so I could minister to hurting people, both saved and unsaved.

On Saturday afternoon my new friend was dismissed from the hospital. When I heard of this, I asked him to testify at the Sunday night rally. It seemed fitting for him to testify publicly when so many people had prayed. He needed to tell others that he had been restored and that the Lord had healed him.

Sunday night the church was packed. The balcony was filled with youth, many of them friends of the one who was to testify. As he told what God had done for him, he pointed his finger up to the balcony and exhorted, "Don't vex the Holy Spirit. It isn't worth it. Get right with God right away." And many did.

He had learned a very hard lesson. At the first we may only be grieving the Holy Spirit by our ignorance. Later on we begin to resist Him if we do not follow His directions. If this continues we quench Him. When He is quenched, He has no other alternative but to become vexed and fight us if He is going to get us to respond in the right manner.

At the close of this chapter, I pass his exhortation on to you: "Don't vex the Holy Spirit. It isn't worth it." Take every step necessary to keep the lines of communication open between you and God. He does not want to take drastic measures to get your attention. But sometimes He must—in answer to somebody's prayers. To avoid this we might pray for ourselves:

> Do I grieve You, blessed Spirit?
>   Do I quench Your power through sin?
> When I do, O God, forgive me,
>   Then cleanse, renew me from within.

Is there something I am missing,
  When I fail to win the lost?
Am I lacking something vital?
  Have I failed to pay the cost?

Have I resisted Your enduement,
  Turning You aside for sin,
'Til You quenched, and vexed forsook me,
  When the tempter came within?

Holy Spirit, come, I pray You;
  Wholly Yours would I be;
Hear me as I humbly beg You,
  Make me Yours, eternally.

—Robert J. Kuglin

Chapter 9

The Problem of Anger

There appear to be two ways Christians handle anger today. One way is to view it as a gift from God for the release of tension and pressure. The other way is to see it as a sin and then let God sanctify us so that anger will not be part of our lives.

Somehow these two views of anger are not able to stand side by side. One view calls it a gift from God. The other view calls it a sin. Certainly God cannot give us a gift of sin and still call Himself God. Either one is wrong and the other is right, or they are both wrong and there is a third alternative.

What should we do therefore with this problem? It is not sufficient for us to shrug our shoulders and hope that it will go away.

I can think of no better place to discuss this major problem than in a book about the Holy Spirit. He has given us the Bible. If the Bible speaks to the issue, then we should look at what the Holy Spirit says about it.

Now there are some things about which the
Bible is silent. In other areas the Bible is clear,
plain and forceful. For example, the Bible tells
me quite forcefully that I am to preach the gospel to all the world. However, it does not specifically tell me how to do it and where specifically
I should go.

But what about anger? Is the Bible specific
about it? What does it say? Is anger a gift from
God for blowing off steam? Is it a sin that requires
confession to God and forgiveness from God and
man? What does the psychologist say? Does the
Bible agree with him?

The words *anger* and *angry* are used over 200
times in the Old Testament. In the majority of
these times they are used to reveal God's anger
with individuals and nations. Excellent examples
of this can be seen by looking at a few representative verses.

Moses said, "The LORD was angry with me because of you, and he solemnly swore that I would
not cross the Jordan . . ." (Deuteronomy 4:21).
Concerning Moses' brother in Deuteronomy 9:20
we read, "And the LORD was angry enough with
Aaron to destroy him . . ."

In First Kings 11:9 we note, "The LORD became
angry with Solomon because his heart had turned
away from the LORD, the God of Israel, who had
appeared to him twice." Further on we see, "So
the LORD was very angry with Israel and removed
them from his presence. Only the tribe of Judah
was left" (2 Kings 17:18).

In all the above verses He is angry at His own people. Of course His anger goes out to other nations as well: "See, the Name of the LORD comes from afar, with burning anger and dense clouds of smoke; his lips are full of wrath, and his tongue is a consuming fire. His breath is like a rushing torrent, rising up to the neck. He shakes the nations in the sieve of destruction . . ." (Isaiah 30:27-28).

There is something else that is very interesting in these anger passages. We have noted that over half of the passages refer to God being angry. I have noticed further that over half of these times, "the LORD'S anger was kindled," or a variation of this clause, is used. Still further, the anger is either "because of" or "against" someone. And in every case He is using His righteous anger to correct a situation.

Let us also look at the word *wrath*. It is used nearly 200 times in the Old Testament. It is sufficient for this study to state that wrath pretty well parallels anger. Also, in the English translations, anger and wrath are used interchangeably.

Some modern psychologists have suggested that anger is an attribute of God just as love is. (I do not find this in the list of attributes given to us by the theologians.) There is a big difference of course. God loves everybody, both sinner and saint, because "God is love" (1 John 4:8). However, God is not angry with everybody. Nowhere in Scripture do we find the statement, "God is anger."

In this the psychologist goes too far. God does not love us because we do good in the same way as

His anger is kindled because we do wrong. There is no parallel. But God does get angry. That is true.

Let us now take a look at Jesus. I have many books on counseling in my library. Many of them are by Christian authors. In almost all of these Christian-oriented books there are statements that show that the writers believe that Jesus showed His anger freely. I believe this completely over-steps what the Bible indicates.

Many times Matthew 23:13-36 is used to show the anger of Jesus as He pronounces woe after woe on the scribes and Pharisees. There may have been scribes and Pharisees in the crowd as Jesus spoke, but the Bible does not tell us. On this the Bible is silent. But what is evident is that He was not giving His address to the scribes and Phari-sees. The whole passage begins with: "Then Jesus said to the crowds and to his disciples: 'The teach-ers of the law and the Pharisees sit in Moses' seat' " (Matthew 23:1).

Jesus was talking about them, not to them. I see no more trace of anger in this passage than there need be when I am issuing a warning from the pulpit to sinners concerning the judgment that is to come upon them.

Although we cannot assume that Jesus' teach-ings are recorded chronologically, it is interesting to note that Matthew concludes the chapter with the sympathetic words, "O Jerusalem, Jerusalem, you who kill the prophets and stone those sent to you, how often I have longed to gather your children together, . . . but you were not willing" (Matthew 23:37).

No. There is no proof that He was angry in Matthew 23.

Another passage of Scripture often used to show that He was angry is John 2:13-17, where Jesus cleansed the temple. Some psychologists say that Jesus became angry and violently overturned the tables. Nowhere does the Scripture say this. They argue from silence and the argument is wrong.

Jesus did make a scourge of small cords. He did drive the sellers and the animals out of the temple. He did pour out the money. He did overthrow the tables. But let us notice a few things. His scourge of small cords could hardly be thought of as an instrument of warfare. The wording indicates that He made the scourge after He saw what was going on. And where did He get the small cords, I might ask, if they were not from the sellers themselves? Yes, He gave them plenty of time to think, and ask themselves what was going on. Any of the sellers could have stopped him or later yanked the scourge from His hand. It was merely a symbolic scourge. It was not a weapon.

Notice that there was no sign of violence. The group of dealers could have easily overpowered Him if He had come in fighting. If He had been violent they would have answered with violence. But how could they fight a man who had not come to fight?

Anger? Fight? That hardly sounds like the One we see in John 7. The temple guards had been sent to capture Jesus. They returned empty-handed with the excuse, "No one ever spoke the was this man does" (John 7:46). No, Jesus was not a fighting man. There is no indication of violence in all His ministry.

Furthermore, the phrase "and drove all from the temple area" (John 2:15), does not indicate that He actively did it. The passage itself says that Jesus talked to them about it, telling them to "Get these out of here!" (2:16). That was typical of Jesus. He got things done by His speaking. I say, as the Bible says, He drove them out with His words, not His whip.

Angry? Those who say so draw from silence. I say He was not angry. A careful reading of the passage indicates that He did it in the way that the Holy Spirit tells us to do it: "But everything should be done in a fitting and orderly way" (1 Corinthians 14:40).

Now we come to the tough one. Mark tells us that when Jesus was healing the man with the paralyzed hand that "He looked around at them in anger and, deeply distressed at their stubborn hearts, . . ." (Mark 3:5).

Hard heartedness means something different today from the meaning of the word in the Bible. To us it may mean cruel or calloused. But to the Hebrew it meant a stubborn resistance to what He knew God wanted. Here we have the same idea that Stephen was talking about in Acts 7:51, with which we have already dealt in chapter 6. They were openly resisting Jesus.

They were stubbornly opposing Jesus. They rebelled. Remember what Samuel said to King Saul? "For rebellion is like the sin of divination, and arrogance like the evil of idolatry" (1 Samuel 15:23). This is what the Son of God had to contend with. Of this event Luke says, "But they were furious and began to discuss with one another what they might do to Jesus" (Luke 6:11).

Nevertheless, Jesus did get angry. The Bible says so. Some Bible commentators say that He cut them all with a condemnatory glance. It was an indignant anger fully consistent with the love and pity He had for them. But there was no action against them, not even a word.

But it was anger. And it is the same word used when the Holy Spirit tells us to put off anger as one of the works of the flesh, "Get rid of all bitterness, rage and anger, brawling and slander, along with every form of malice" (Ephesians 4:31).

Many Bible commentators avoid the matter of Jesus' anger, either in whole or in part. Most Christian psychologists jump on Mark 3:5 as a proof text to show that anger is a very good thing. They almost make it a part of the fruit of the Spirit. I will go to neither extreme.

Some more observations will shed understanding on the situation. Jesus is being condemned for working on the Sabbath day. But He was not working. He merely spoke a few words in this instance, "Stretch out your hand" (3:5b). He had not broken a law at all.

But the Pharisees plotted to kill him. They had an executive meeting on the Sabbath. They broke the fourth commandment, "Remember the Sabbath day by keeping it holy," with the intention of breaking the sixth commandment, "You shall not murder."

Now remember that Jesus was not only man, but also God, the God-man, God in the flesh. As God He could not help but be angry against them. His anger was kindled. He was grieved. Does this not tie into our previous chapter on vexing the Holy Spirit? The Holy Spirit can be so grieved and vexed that He fights against people. Jesus became vexed and therefore, as God, as the God we see in the Old Testament, He became angry.

Now does one text, and only one text, an exceptional case, give us the privilege of being angry any time we feel like it? We have already noted that we are not to use a single text in isolation. Further, we need to be careful. We are not God. And God can do some things that we cannot. Have you ever thought of that?

God tells us, "You shall not murder" (Exodus 20:13). But does He set the example? No. We see Him kill people by the thousands in the Old Testament. How many Egyptians did He kill when He piled the waters of the Red Sea upon them? It was an army capable of overtaking about 3 million Israelites.

When the sons of Korah rebelled against God and against Moses and Aaron, God opened up the ground and 250 men were killed as stated in Numbers 16:35. Then next day another 14,700 people died in a judgment-plague (16:49). Are we allowed to kill 14,950 people just because they rebel and complain? No. God kills. But to us He says, "You shall not murder."

There are many other cases throughout the Old Testament. But let us clinch this in our minds simply by direct statements: "See now that I myself am He! There is no god besides me. I put to death and I bring to life, I have wounded and I will heal, and no one can deliver out of my hand" (Deuteronomy 32:39). "The LORD brings death and makes alive; he brings down to the grave and raises up" (1 Samuel 2:6). In the story of Naaman, the king of Israel said, "Am I God? Can I kill and bring back to life?" (2 Kings 5:7).

Just as there are things God does that we may not do, He also tells us to do things that He does not do. He tells us to honor our parents. God does not even have parents. He tells us, "be fruitful and increase in number; fill the earth and subdue it. Rule over the fish of the sea and the birds of the air and over every living creature that moves on the ground" (Genesis 1:28). All this He asks us to do, and yet He does none of these things to set the example.

God created man in His own likeness. Yet He forbids us from making "an idol in the form of anything in heaven above or on the earth beneath or in the waters below" (Exodus 20:4).

Yes, God can do things that He absolutely forbids man to do. Can I suggest at this point that God can become angry, but He absolutely commands us to refrain from anger?

There are a number of words used for anger and different shades of anger in the New Testament. I will mention a couple of them. They may not have much bearing on the question at issue, but we need to know that there is a difference.

In John 7:23 Jesus is asking, ". . . why are you angry with me for healing the whole man on the Sabbath?" The Greek word for anger here is *chalao*, from which we get our word cholera. It means to be full of bile. Jesus is actually asking, "Are you full of bile at Me?" This word is used only once, and that referring to highly aggravated adversaries.

Another word is *thumos* which is used seventeen times and always for wrath or a variation of wrath. An example is in Acts 19:28 where the pagan Ephesians were so upset that the whole city was in an uproar because of Paul's preaching: "When they heard this, they were furious and began shouting: . . ." We are exhorted to lay aside this type of wrath with the other works of the flesh, "sexual immorality, impurity and debauchery; idolatry and witchcraft; hatred, discord, jealousy, fits of rage, selfish ambition, dissensions, factions and envy; drunkenness, orgies, and the like" (Galatians 5:19-21).

Still another word is *thumoomai*, a form of *thumos*. Herod is the single example of this. "When Herod realized that he had been outwitted by the Magi, he was furious, and he gave orders to kill all the boys in Bethlehem . . ." (Matthew 2:16). I am sure no Christian would want to follow Herod's example.

Forty-one other times in Scripture, the word *orge* or a variation of it, is used for anger or a form of anger. A number of other words use *orge* as a root. I am including them in the study, since they too have a bearing on our attitudes toward the Holy Spirit, who He is and what He says.

In order to compare the various words used to designate anger, I constructed the following chart. It will help us to see anger and wrath in proper perspective. Read through the chart, noticing the trends, and refer back to it when I comment on it later. (See chart on next page.)

In drawing up this chart, I took into consideration every verse that speaks of anger and wrath in the New Testament in the English language. Then I also took every verse where the Greek indicated anger or wrath, but the translators elected to use a different word than anger or wrath.

Next I eliminated all the duplicate verses by selecting a representative verse. This I did in the original language. However, some verses with *orge* were translated differently in the English. When this happened I allowed that verse in the chart as well. For example, in Revelation 14:10, *orge* is translated "fury," but in 19:15 it is translated "wrath."

Also we may note that *thumon* is translated both "wrath" and "fierceness." We have the same type

CHART ON GREEK WORDS FOR WRATH AND ANGER

TEXT	THE ENGLISH TRANSLATION	GREEK WORD USED		THE MEANING
Matthew 2:16	[Herod] was furious, and he gave orders to kill	Orgisomenos	thumoothe	to be wroth
Matthew 5:22	I tell you that anyone who is angry with his	orgisthis		to be angry
Matthew 18:34	In anger his master turned him over	orges		to become angry
Mark 3:5	He looked around at them in anger	orgisthis		anger
Luke 14:21	Then the owner of the house became angry and ordered	orgisthe		to become angry
Luke 15:28	Older brother became angry and refused	orge		to be angry
John 3:36	Will not see life			anger, wrath
John 7:23	Are you angry with me		cholate	to be filled with bile
Romans 10:19	By those who are not a nation; I will make you angry	parorgion		to make angry
Romans 12:19	But leave room for God's wrath	orge	thumoy	anger, wrath
Galatians 5:20	Hatred, discord, jealousy, fits of rage, factions			mind, wrath
Ephesians 4:26	In your anger do not sin	orgisesthe		to be angry
Ephesians 4:26	Do not let the sun go down while you are still angry	parorgismo		a provoking to anger
Ephesians 4:31	Get rid of all bitterness, rage		thumos	mind, wrath
Ephesians 4:31	And anger	orge		anger, wrath
Ephesians 6:4	Do not exasperate your children; instead, bring	parorgisete		to anger beyond measure
Colossians 3:8	Rid yourselves of all such things as these: anger, rage, malice		thumon	mind, wrath
I Timothy 2:8	Lift up holy hands in prayer, without anger or disputing	orges		anger, wrath
Titus 1:7	An overseer must be...not quick-tempered, not given	orgilon		prone to anger, passionate
James 1:19	Slow to speak and slow to become angry	orge		anger, wrath
Revelation 14:10	Drink of the wine of God's fury		thumon	mind, wrath
Revelation 14:10	Into the cup of his wrath	orge		anger, wrath
Revelation 19:15	Tread the winepress of the fury		thumos	mind, wrath
Revelation 19:15	Of the wrath of God Almighty	orge		anger, wrath

of thing with *orgisthis*, being translated as "fury" in one place and "wrath" in another. This latter should not have been permitted in Matthew 18:34, since it means to become angry, but does not mean wrath at all.

At a glance it is easy to see that there are really only four words used in the original: *orge, thumoo, chalao* and *thumos*. Everything else on the chart is a variation mostly due to changes necessary for verbal construction, and also for the intensity required for the verb in a certain circumstance.

There are many other verses using some of these words. But I singled everything down to one. Even if there appears to be a duplication, a closer look will reveal that there are absolutely no total duplications.

There is only one place in all the New Testament where *thumos* is used, and that brought about the murder of children. There is only one place that *chalao* is used and that is an anger that turns to hate. The Holy Spirit saw no reason to direct us away from these. It is plain without any admonition.

There is only one clear indication that Jesus was ever angry, and I have already dealt with that. There is only one place where we are told that a Christian is to be angry. Notice that ten times in the chart we are told to get rid of anger and wrath. These are only representative of many verses where we are to do so, either by command or inference. Then we have that one verse that sticks out like a sore thumb.

It is the first part of Ephesians 4:26: "In your anger do not sin."

In 1953 I was asked to give a lecture to ministers on the inspiration of the Bible. I made the immature statement that if anyone could show me a contradiction, I would not only eat the page on which it was recorded, but I would eat the whole book. A liberal theologian remarked out loud, "Somebody go for catsup." Then came that cutthroat question and answer time at the end. I took all the questions and answered them from God's inspired Word. And I did not need the catsup. Some men of the cloth came to realize that there may be some tensions in the Bible. But contradictions, there are none.

However, if they had asked me to reconcile "In your anger" with "Get rid of all . . . anger" I would have been dumbfounded at that time. I would have had no answer. They are complete opposites. Even the verb *to be angry* comes from the same root as *anger*. One cannot even say that they are really different words.

In some psychological writings, it is claimed that "Be ye angry" (4:26, KJV) is a command. It is further stated that "let all" (4:31, KJV) is something that we may do if we desire. Therefore, it is claimed, the former verse is much stronger than the latter. This is a very poor argument. *Orgisesthe* in 4:26 is the permissive imperative, not a command at all. Actually it is the forbidding of sinning, as the danger in anger.

Then in 4:31, "be put away" (KJV) is in the first aorist passive imperative, meaning to pick up, carry away and make a clean sweep. In other words, get rid of anger forever.

However, does a person have to know Greek and all its intricacies in order to understand the Bible? Can a lay person not know truth? Yes indeed, and there is a simple answer to all of this. But the simple answer may lead to further problems—at least it will lead to other questions.

Almost any Bible with a reference margin will direct you to Psalm 4:4; "In your anger do not sin; when you are on your beds, search your hearts and be silent. *Selah*." Look at your own reference Bible and see if it does not direct you to this psalm.

Why the reference to Psalm 4:4? At first glance the verses do not look much alike, but they really are. Let us take them one half at a time and line them up one above the other. The first couplet looks like this:

Ephesians 4:26:	In your anger do not sin.
Psalm 4:4:	In your anger do not sin.

The second couplet looks like this:

Ephesians 4:26:	Do not let the sun go down while you are still angry.
Psalm 4:4:	When you are on your beds

Do you see the similarity? Even in the second couplet Paul tells us that we are not to let the night come without getting rid of our anger. David tells us that when we go to bed, we ought to go quietly and be in peace. And he adds, "Selah," which may well mean "Stop and think of that."

There is another good reason for lining them up, besides the obvious similarities. Almost every commentator you turn to will tell you that Paul quotes Psalm 4:4 exactly, but that he does it from the Septuagint version, not from the Hebrew text.[1] Herein is the problem. It just did not come out the same. The only commentators that do not so state are the ones that avoid the problem altogether.

"Stand in awe" means to be afraid, be moved, quake or tremble. It has nothing at all to do with being angry. It is the "I am astounded!" of today. And if this astounding makes you angry, do not go to bed with your anger. Put it away.

I have written at length about anger. Why? I have said very little in this chapter so far about the Holy Spirit. Really, it all leads into something very crucial concerning the working of the Holy Spirit. (See chart on next page.)

Anger is just about as bad a sin as anyone can commit. There are no good sins, but some are worse than others. Personally, I cannot think of a worse one than anger, except it be the result of anger.

Let us return to the fruit of the Spirit which is "love, joy, peace, patience, kindness, goodness, faithfulness, gentleness and self-control" (Galatians 5:22-23). All of this, the Spirit-filled Christian will be manifesting in his life. The following chart will enable you to see the effects of anger on the fruit of the Spirit.

When we allow anger to take over, love is put out. Anger develops hate, not love. When we al-

A   Love
                               Joy
N   Peace
                      Long-suffering
G   Gentleness
                       Goodness
E   Faith
                       Meekness
R   Self-control

low anger to take over, joy is put out. Happy and mad do not mix.

When we allow anger to take over, peace is gone. I have yet to see an angry person showing peace of heart. If he is prone to anger, the peace generally does not show even if he says he has peace. When we allow anger to take hold of us, it shows a lack of patience or long-suffering.

When we allow anger in our lives, gentleness flees. When we allow anger to take over, what happens to goodness? It goes too. "Oh," you say, "I caught you on faith." No indeed. Have you ever seen a person who is angry down on his knees praying and showing great faith in God?

Meekness? Moses was the meekest man on the face of the earth (Numbers 12:3, KJV). Yet he was angry on a number of occasions. But he was not meek and angry at the same time. And every time he became angry he was judged for it. Even when Moses had a good excuse to become angry, he was punished for it. When he came down from the mountain and saw the children of Israel streak dancing around their newly made idol-calf, he lost his temper and broke the tablets of stone because the Israelites had broken the first commandment which he carried. "You shall have no other gods before me" (Exodus 20:3). They had also broken the second commandment, "You shall not make for yourself an idol in the form of anything in heaven above or on the earth beneath or in the waters below. You shall not bow down to them or worship them; for I, the LORD your God, am a jealous God, punishing the children for the sin of the fathers to the third and fourth generation of those who hate me, but showing love to a thousand generations of those who love me and keep my commandments" (Exodus 20:4-6).

Now Moses was called to go up the mountain a second time. God would again write the commandments with His own finger. But this time Moses had to make the stones himself and carry them up the mountain (Deuteronomy 10:1). Now it is a lot easier to carry stones down a mountain than to carry stones up a mountain. I think, at every step, Moses would be thinking, *I have to do this because I got mad.*

Concerning the ninth flavor of the fruit of the Spirit, self-control already went out so anger could come in. If we are Spirit-filled there will be no room for anger in our lives. Self-control being part of the fruit rules out the possibility of having anger in us to control us.

Do you see it now? Anger will drive out every flavor of the fruit of the Spirit with one foul blow. That is why it is such a terrible sin. I can think of no other sin that causes so much trouble, even to the extent that it brings on killings.

Today we are told that if we do not release anger, our bodies remain ready for action. It is a time when people have heart attacks. Many medical problems are cited as the result of pent-up anger. All of this is true. But that does not say that it is God's method any more than abortion is God's method to keep the population down.

We need to recognize it as a heinous sin and ask forgiveness. Then we need to immediately ask the Holy Spirit to fill us so there will not be room in us for anger to dwell.

Remember that instead of anger the Scriptures tell us that we are to forgive "seventy-seven times" (Matthew 18:22). Jesus said it. And I believe it.

And He has left us an example: "He was oppressed and afflicted, yet he did not open his mouth; he was led like a lamb to the slaughter, and as a sheep before her shearers is silent, so he did not open his mouth" (Isaiah 53:7). "When they hurled their insults at him, he did not retaliate; when he suffered, he made no threats. Instead, he entrusted himself to him who judges justly" (1 Peter 2:23).

Anger is a terrible, terrible thing. I can think of no faster way to grieve and quench the Holy Spirit than by our anger. Let us get rid of it. Yes. Make a clean sweep of it. A good start would be by praying:

More holiness give me,
　　More strivings within,
More patience in suffering,
　　More sorrow for sin,
More faith in my Saviour,
　　More sense of His care,
More joy in His service,
　　More purpose in prayer.

More gratitude give me,
　　More trust in the Lord,
More pride in His glory,
　　More hope in His Word;
More tears for His sorrows,
　　More pain at His grief;
More meekness in trial,
　　More praise for relief.

More purity give me,
　　More strength to o'ercome;
More freedom from earth stains,
　　More longings for home;
More fit for the kingdom,
　　More used wouldI be;
More blessed and holy—
　　More, Saviour like Thee.

—Philip P. Bliss

Endnotes

1. The Septuagint is the oldest Greek translation of the Old Testament, written before the time of Christ. It is thought that Ptolemy II of Egypt brought seventy scholars from Alexandria to complete the translation from the Hebrew in seventy days. The most famous translations are the Vaticanus in Rome, and the Alexandinus and the Sinaiticus in London.

Chapter 10

Slain in the Spirit

Being slain in the Spirit is not a new phenomenon. Accounts of the great revivals in the United States in the time of Charles E. Finney confirm this. But although each denomination denied there was any barking like dogs and slaying in the Spirit in its own denomination, they accused other denominations of having these things happen in theirs.

One night as the elders and I were praying for a lady in a meeting in New Jersey, she collapsed and appeared to be unconscious. Somebody nearby exclaimed, "Slain in the Spirit!"

I answered, "I think not."

It certainly did not resemble anything like I had heard about being so slain. Some of my sources were quite sympathetic. Others were antagonistic. However, I for one was open to all that the Holy Spirit has for the Christian in these days. What I really needed was some firsthand information or experience in order to make a proper assessment. I had heard a number of people condemn this exotic experience, although they had only passed judgment by hearsay.

In a minute or so the lady was back to normal. Well, better than normal. She had been ill and under a doctor's care for some time. Now she was perfectly well, as attested by her doctor some time later. God had put her to sleep, just as He did Adam, and healed her in her sleep. Why? I do not know, except that it is one of God's many methods in healing.

Shortly afterward, I was the speaker in another crusade in another area. Here I would be able to gain prime experience. The pastor not only encouraged being slain in the Spirit, it was practiced. Indeed a service was not a total service unless this manifestation was present.

Besides observing the practice, I also took a new look at the Word of God, with the assistance of many who were enjoying these occurrences. I had to remember that I was there to build up the church, not cause trouble. Therefore, even though I questioned, I was making "every effort to keep the unity of the Spirit through the bond of peace" (Ephesians 4:3), which the people appeared to be experiencing.

Biblical references upon which to base my understanding were not numerous, but there were some. Moses "fell prostrate before the Lord" (Deuteronomy 9:18). Looking up the verse for the complete context, I found that it continued a little further with, "for forty days and forty nights; I ate no bread and drank no water, because of all the sin you had commited, doing what was evil in the LORD'S sight and so provoking him to anger."

I recognized that Moses went down before the LORD because of the sin of the people. And he fasted and prayed. This was not exactly what these people were doing in the meetings. However, if what happened to them was the same as what happened to Moses, then it was a good verse to use.

However the Bible was silent as to how Moses "fell prostrate." I could not persuade them that Moses merely kneeled down before the LORD just as I had done so many times. Neither could they persuade me that Moses fell onto his back for an extended period of time. No. This did not appear to fit.

Ezra also fell down before the LORD. No. This did not appear to fit. This was good again. He wrote, "Then, at the evening sacrifice, I rose from my self-abasement . . ." (sounds like an evening service) ". . . with my tunic and cloak torn, and fell on my knees with my hands spread out to the LORD my God" (Ezra 9:5).

Like Ezra, I had often been down on my knees with my hands spread in praise and prayer to God. But I had never called it "slain in the Spirit." But then I had never called it anything. I had no name for it at all. At least these people called it something. However, Ezra's actions did not even come close to what these people were doing. This did not fit either.

In two passages in Daniel we read about Daniel and Nebuchadnezzar falling on their faces. Daniel says, "I was terrified and fell prostrate. . . . I was in a deep sleep, with my face to the ground . . ." (Daniel 8:17-18). That sounded more like it except that my new friends always fell on their backs.

But I could not presume that whether one fell frontward or backward made that much difference. The pastor said that it was for decency's sake. Good enough.

On a number of interviews I was directed to Isaiah 28. Most knew the phraseology but did not know where the verses were found. "Very well then, with foreign lips and strange tongue God will speak to this peopl.e . . . This is the resting place. . . . The word of the LORD to them will become . . . so that they will go and fall backward" (Isaiah 28:11-13).

This really sounded like it might fit a little better than the other verses. However, the verse concludes like this: "and fall backward, be injured and snared and captured" (28:13). The whole picture is that of the Assyrian army overtaking a people that would not learn to do what God wanted them to do.

In John 18:3, Judas came "guiding a detachment of soldiers. . . . They were carrying torches, lanterns and weapons" to betray Jesus. Verse six says, "When Jesus said, 'I am he,' they drew back and fell to the ground."

We may have no doubt here. They certainly fell backward. The big problem is that they were haters of the Lord Jesus Christ. They were coming to capture Him, not worship Him.

I tried the conversion of Saul of Tarsus for size. He was on the road to Damascus, with letters that gave him authority to persecute the saints. Then a sudden burst of "light from heaven flashed around him. He fell to the ground and heard a voice say to him, 'Saul, Saul, why do you persecute me?' " (Acts 9:3-4). This account is repeated in Acts 22:6-7 and 26:13-14, to give it a three-fold impact.

Paul was one of the most terrible persecutors of the church. He certainly was not worshiping God. God had to knock him down to get his attention. Why? Because the Holy Spirit was vexed, not because He was being worshiped.

From this I concluded that there was a certain falling down before the Lord, three times attested. But the case cited was for sinners, not saints. Paul picks this up again in First Corinthians 14:24-25, in the chapter that directs us in the use of prophecy, tongues and the interpretation of tongues: "But if an unbeliever or someone who does not understand comes in . . . he will fall down and worship God, . . ."

Consider the experience of another great apostle, Peter. "About noon . . . Peter went up on the roof to pray. . . . he fell into a trance. He saw heaven opened . . ." (Acts 10:9-11). Here was a saint. He was at prayer. He fell into a trance, in what position we do not know. We do know that he was not standing because verse 13 tells us "Get up, Peter. Kill and eat."

Peter calls this a vision twice (10:17, 19), and then gives two further indications that it was

(10:11, 30). Of all the people I talked to who had been "slain in the Spirit," none had had a vision during that time. It was a silent and dark mystery. They could not describe it. Peter could.

When the wise men came to Jerusalem to see Jesus, "On coming to the house, they saw the child with his mother Mary, and they bowed down and worshiped him. Then they opened their treasures and presented him with gifts of gold and of incense and of myrrh" (Matthew 2:11). Obviously here, they were not out cold on their backs. They were carrying gifts to give to the King of kings and Lord of lords.

In Genesis 17:3 we read that Abraham "fell facedown, and God said to him, . . ." This I believe God wants us all to do. Mary did so in John 11:32, as did a certain woman in Mark 7:25 and a number of others throughout the Scriptures.

How different this is from the meeting at which I was invited to speak. There, everyone fell backward. Generally it was when the pastor placed his hand on their foreheads and prayed for them. As a rule he gave them a little push backward, being careful to ensure there was a catcher right there.

I noticed that all catchers were men. Nearly everyone who fell down was a woman, although a few men did so too. It happened almost every night to the same people. They seemed to be the select, and sometimes they slighted others who were not quite "with it."

There was something else I noticed. Women with slacks or jeans could be slain almost any place. Women with skirts and dresses always went to one corner of the church and waited for the pastor to come so they could be slain. This was the place where the blankets were available to cover their bare legs when dresses drew up higher than propriety allowed.

That there were some unique experiences I cannot deny. One young lady remained out cold far longer than anybody else. She was usually one of the first to go down, and almost always the last to get up. One night I took her by the arm to see if she were conscious. She was cold and rigid. When I lifted her arm, her whole shoulder and side came up with her arm. When I tried the same with her foot, the whole bottom part of her body had to be lifted as well. She was like a hardwood plank.

Later I asked her what went on when she was slain. She replied "It is just so wonderful!" When I asked her to explain what her statement meant she said that she really could not tell. Finally she admitted that she could remember absolutely nothing from the time the pastor prayed until she came to again. She did not know that I had lifted her.

So her experience was real. But real what, I was not too sure at the time. I needed to investigate a little more.

There were others that faked it. One young man went down almost every night with a smile on his face. But every once in a while he would open an eye to see how things were going. When he discovered that I was watching him, he quickly closed it again.

No one was able to tell me of any concrete experience except that they had been slain in the Spirit. They admitted that it brought no change to their lives. They were not empowered for service. It was only an experience that was an end in itself.

I challenged a few of them to stop falling down on the floor so that they would be able to help me pray with people that needed help. I told them, "If I fell onto the floor and became unconscious every time somebody prayed for me, I would hardly ever get to preach." There was an immediate change. Some of them never fell down again. I have talked to a few of them since that time. They have never gone down since, and have thanked me for my advice. Others, of course, just became more determined than ever and continued the practice.

I looked into the Scriptures again after all my investigation to see if there might be something I had been missing. I read the Bible completely through within a week with but one purpose in mind. I wanted to see if the Bible really spoke to this question.

The only thing that I could come up with that came close to describing the case of rigidity and the other happenings was in Mark 9:14-29 where Jesus was casting the demon out of the boy: "The boy looked so much like a corpse that many said, 'He's dead' " (9:26). It reminded me of the pastor's statement in describing some of the parishioners who fell down and became rigid. He said, "They are like dead people. One must die to self, you know."

It all appeared to me to be a complete violation of the Scriptures. I was sure I was observing the power of evil spirits and not the power of the Holy Spirit at all.

I have been very careful in my ministry to endeavor to keep from grieving the Holy Spirit. I think that it is a terrible thing to ascribe to the devil that which the Holy Spirit is doing. This is called blasphemy (Matthew 12:31). But I do know that we have the world, the flesh and the devil to contend with. And a lot of what I saw was at least a work of the flesh, and maybe a little worse.

Many years ago three young aspiring preachers and I were prayed for at the Annual Council of The Christian and Missionary Alliance. As the brother prayed for us, the three buckled at the knees and went down. Only I remained upright. For a number of days I felt depressed. I reasoned this way, "They received the power of God and I got nothing." I examined my heart. "Had I grieved, resisted, quenched or vexed the Holy Spirit?" Then over a period of months I received the news all three of my buddies had left the ministry. Was it because of that one event? I do not know. But this I do know: I have continued in an ever-expanding ministry that has taken me all across North America and to the Philippines, Hong Kong, China, Japan, India and New Zealand. There have been calls from many other countries as well.

The Bible tells us that we are to try the spirits in First John 4:1: "Dear friends, do not believe every spirit, but test the spirits to see whether they are from God, because many false prophets have gone out into the world."

Is "slaying in the Spirit" a work of the Holy Spirit or not? Does it come from a contrary source? You have read about my own investigation of the subject. Now you be the judge for yourself.

The church needs men and women, filled with the Holy Spirit, who have the gift of the discerning of spirits. The spirit of antichrist is already in the world (1 John 4:3). At a time like this we need not only to sing some of our hymns but to pray them.

Open my eyes that I may see
    Glimpses of truth Thou hast for me;
Place in my hands the wonderful key
    That shall unclasp and set me free.

Open my mind that I may read
    More of Thy love in word and deed.
What shall I fear while yet Thou dost
    lead?
Only for light from Thee I plead.

Open my way that I may bring
    Trophies of grace to Christ, my King;
Echoed in love Thy word shall outring,
    Sweet as the note that angels sing.

Silently now I wait for Thee,
   Ready, my God, Thy will to see;
Open my eyes, illumine me,
   Spirit divine!

—Clara H. Scott

Chapter 11

The Spirit's Gifts to Man

In the first of the three special chapters on the Holy Spirit, First Corinthians 12, 13 and 14, we are told that "the manifestation of the Spirit is given for the common good . . ." (12:7).

When I ask the question, "What is the manifestation of the Spirit?" in a class where I am almost a stranger, I get one of two answers as a rule.

One is a very enthusiastic, "It is tongues." The other answer is almost complete silence. It is an icy silence that says, "Oh, no. What kind of an evangelist is this?"

The two answers are almost identical. One says the manifestation is tongues. The other says in effect, "He wants us to say that it is tongues. If we do not say 'tongues' then we have nothing to say."

The Bible interprets itself if we will read far enough. Notice the connecting word "for" in verse 8, KJV. It connects "the manifestation" of verse 7 with the way the Holy Spirit is manifested in our living according to verses 8 to 10. So at last we have reached the manifestations of the Spirit. Let us see what they are.

Wisdom. Many times in Bible discussions I have been asked my opinion of certain gifts, generally the gift of tongues. Sometimes it will be miracles of healing, but seldom anything beyond this. It is my custom to answer, "Well, let us start at the top and work down to that one." Then there is usually silence. Then I will add, "The top one, the best one, is wisdom. At least it is at the first of the list." (See chart, page 65.)

I believe it to be the best one. This is readily seen as we continue. But "let us have a discussion about wisdom," will usually generate nothing more than silence.

First Corinthians 12:11 says, "he gives them to each one, just as he determines." It is therefore generally held that we should not ask for any of the gifts since the Holy Spirit will give us what He knows we need. A gift is a gift. It is something that is given, not something for which we ask.

But if we are not to ask for any of the gifts at all, it becomes very difficult to put into practice a few things that God orders us to do. If the Holy Spirit tells us to ask for one of the gifts, even though He also tells us that He gives them as He desires, then it is plain that He wants us to have it and He also wants us to ask for it. James 1:5 says, "If any of you lacks wisdom, he should ask God, who gives generously to all without finding fault, and it will be given to him." The Bible says we are to ask for wisdom, and God will not even scold us for our asking.

Paul tells us that we are to walk as wise men and know what the will of the Lord is (Ephesians 5:15-17). Then in Colossians he prays for the saints, saying that he has "not stopped praying for you and asking God to fill you with the knowledge of his will through all spiritual wisdom and understanding" (Colossians 1:9).

Solomon, the man of wisdom, put it this way: "Get wisdom, get understanding. . . . Do not forsake wisdom, and she will protect you; love her, and she will watch over you. Wisdom is supreme" (Proverbs 4:5-7). He says also, "He who gets wisdom loves his own soul" (19:8), and "he who wins souls is wise" (11:30).

This is why I put wisdom at the top of the gifts of the Spirit, not just because it comes first in the biblical listing. We are ordered to have it. We are commanded to ask for it if we do not have it. We are told that it is the principal thing, the best.

How will we know when we have it? The last little sentence in Matthew 11:19 tells us: "But wisdom is proved right by her actions." In other words we will know we have wisdom when we stop making the many mistakes that seem to come so naturally to us.

Wisdom on church boards would effectively eliminate many small churches. They would all know exactly what God wanted the people to do to get the church producing. Did we not notice that winning souls comes with wisdom?

Wisdom is also a very quiet manifestation. Oh, that many Christians would ask for it! Look at a church full of wisdom. No gossip. No mistakes. Every one winning souls. Every one knowing what to do with the new converts. What a church!

Knowledge. With knowledge, there are two prominent opinions. One states that it comes to us through the study of the Word of God. However, we need to note that it is a gift, not something we gain by earning or learning. And it is a gift for Christians, not everyone. I know of a considerable number of people who have a large knowledge of God's Word who openly oppose Christianity.

The gift of knowledge is simply knowing things. God tells the one so gifted, and there is no other explanation. Peter was given knowledge when he faced Ananias concerning the sale of some property. Peter just knew that Ananias was lying: "Ananias, how is it that Satan has so filled your heart that you have lied to the Holy Spirit. . . . You have not lied to men but to God" (Acts 5:3-4). How did Peter know? God told him. It is the gift of knowing.

Three hours later Sapphira came in. Peter knew that she had connived with her husband in the matter. Then he used his gift of prophecy as well. He stated that the young men "will carry you out" (Acts 5:9). She fell down immediately. Wouldn't Peter have looked stupid if she had lived for another thirty years? He knew what had happened. And he knew what was going to happen.

Nowhere are we exhorted to ask for this gift although we are told to add learning to our repertoire. In fact, it is doubtful that the Holy Spirit would give it to anyone unless they first of all had wisdom in order to use it properly.

Faith. Here is another gift that we need to ask for if we do not have it, because "without faith it is impossible to please God" (Hebrews 11:6). God does not ask us to do that which He does not make possible. Therefore He had a gift to make it possible for us to please Him.

A man I knew was looking for a church so he could attend a midweek service while traveling in the state of Ohio. He found a small church with a few cars around it. He was late, and the group was about to go to prayer for a special need just as he arrived. He told the pastor that he knew that he was a guest, but he believed that he had the gift of faith from the Holy Spirit. He wondered if he might lead the congregation in prayer. "Praise the Lord," exclaimed the pastor. "We need $75,000 by tomorrow noon. If we do not get it, we will lose our building."

That would be enough to make most visitors sit down very quickly. But this man prayed instead. The next morning an elderly lady arrived at the church office. She wanted to know who should look after her check for $75,000. The Lord had spoken to her the previous evening about 8:30 p.m. She was sorry she could not get it to them any sooner.

Faith is another gift that we can ask for, and need to ask for.

Healings. Paul exemplified this in the account concerning Publius' father. "Paul went in to see him and, after prayer, placed his hands on him and healed him" (Acts 28:8). Some writers will tell us that all miracles, healings, etc., ceased halfway through Acts. Do not believe it: "Jesus Christ is the same yesterday and today and forever" (Hebrews 13:8).

A similar thing happened in Acts 3:1-8, when "a man crippled from birth . . . went with them into the temple courts, walking and jumping, and praising God." Peter and John did not even pray. They simply commanded the man, "In the name of Jesus Christ of Nazareth, walk."

Many people can attest to this ministry today, including me. I was crippled in the mid-1960s and considered totally disabled while suffering excruciating pain. I am now able to do all my work and traveling without any pain. God has straightened out my body. He has lengthened my left leg which had shrunk two-and-one-half inches. He has given me full use of all my limbs. He cured me of sarcoidosis of the lungs and completely delivered me from periods of total blindness with terrible headaches.

It appears to me that the healing really started when two men came to visit me in the Ottawa Civic Hospital the Sunday afternoon before I was scheduled for surgery. They both laid their hands on me as they prayed. Many others had prayed much during the years preceding this with little or no relief.

There is no place in the Scriptures where we are exhorted to ask for this ministry in particular. The same can be said for the one following.

Miracles. You might call healing the working of miracles. But healings, of course, involve our bodies; miracles do not have to refer to our bodies at all, so there is a difference.

I recall a very devoted couple who began farming in an area which depended on irrigation. The local farmers used the old way of irrigating, the ditch method, whereby they flooded their land by overflowing the ditches onto their acreages. It was the only way they could get a crop. Rain was rare in the summer.

At their very first irrigation association meeting, the newly arrived couple informed the organization that they would not take any water on the Lord's Day. Any other day was acceptable, but they kept the Lord's Day for rest. The others laughed with scorn, but my friends would not recant. You may have guessed some of the rest. The association planned it so the Christian couple could only get water on Sundays, or not at all.

My friends prayed that God would vindicate Himself and the testimony of His people. Nothing happened. The neighbors on all sides had good crops coming along. Lush fields of prairie wheat, six, eight, ten inches high, looking like well cared for lawns of green. Then came the most severe hailstorm on record for the area. It wiped out every farmer except my friends, two of God's saints.

They had nothing to lose. Nothing had come up. But with up to a foot of hail melting on their land, the seed began to germinate. They had the only crop in the entire area. The age of miracles is not past. There are those who still have the gift.

Prophecy. I touched on this gift when I mentioned Peter and Sapphira. Many maintain that prophecy either is not with us anymore, or that it is merely the preaching of God's Word. Others say that prophecy in the Old Testament was *foretelling*, and prophecy in the New Testament is *forthtelling*.

To all of these ideas, I simply ask, "If God decided to change His mind, why didn't He tell us He would, instead of telling us He would not?" I find that the prophet in the Old Testament not only foretold, but also preached. Jonah's sermon should have been taped. God used it to turn a city of about one million to Himself. Why should there be any change in the New Testament?

This gift of prophecy was used by a man to launch me into a new and enlarged ministry of evangelism. One of my overseers gave me special direction for the Lord's work in January of 1972. He told me that I was to go to Dunedin, Florida. I was to go to Trinity Bible College and ask for either Mrs. McLean or Dr. John Minder. This seemed a little far-fetched to me. I lived over 1,000 miles from Florida and I had no money. But it was prophetic. It was a word from the Lord through a man who had recently met the Lord in a new way.

Within two weeks I was in Florida with my wife and her parents. I went up to the desk at Trinity, and told the charming lady at the switchboard that I was to ask for either Mrs. McLean or Dr. Minder.

The elderly lady said, "I am Mrs. McLean." And a tall, mature gentleman turned around and said, "I'm John Minder." I could hardly believe it. Not only did my adviser have the names correct, but the Lord had it arranged so that I would not have to look for them.

After I had explained to them how it happened that I was there, I asked if they had a room for me for a few weeks. I was told that they were sorry, but they just did not have a room for me.

"I need not press you then," I said. "I have my wife and her parents with me. If you do not have room for one couple you obviously would have a hard time finding rooms for two couples. It is strange that everything has worked out according to the prophecy right up until now. Now there is this dead end."

"It is stranger than you think," responded Mrs. McLean. "We do have room for four, but we do not have room for two. We have a suite for two couples who know each other well. It is the Billy Graham suite. This is the college he attended, you know."

No, I had not known that. It all sounded so impossible. Surely God had something very special arranged besides just a place to stay for a rest. It was fantastic!

Up to this time my ministry had been to small, struggling churches, sometimes in remote areas of Canada. When I was able to get them working for the Lord, I would resign and take on another one in similar straits. Doing this, my world got smaller and smaller, instead of larger and larger, so that I did not know very many of God's great men.

I had never heard of Dr. John Minder. I did not know that he had pastored the great Tampa Gospel Tabernacle for many years until his retirement. I did not know that Billy Graham had been his assistant. And I did not know that Dr. Minder had a particular ministry of steering young men of God in the right direction.

Now God would use him to direct me into a different ministry, a larger one than I had ever enjoyed. He arranged for me to attend the Alliance Church in Dunedin and introduced me to the pastor, Rev. Arlie McGarvey.

That night revival, like the one on the Canadian prairies, broke out in the church that was meeting in the Masonic hall. Dr. Minder saw to it that the auditorium was packed with Trinity students. From there the revival spread to Trinity Bible College, which later provided me with teams of witnessing youths to travel to nearby cities.

At the college the students prayed all night, confessed their sins and made restitutions. They got thoroughly right with God and man. The revival spread to the Tampa Fellowship church and then many other Florida churches experienced an awakening. The results were felt into Georgia and even up into North Carolina.

Soon after that I resigned my last pastorate in Canada, and I have traveled as an evangelist ever since. The gift of prophecy was used by the Lord to steer me.

Discerning of spirits. This gift is very often mis-named and misrepresented as the gift of discern-ment. There is no gift called discernment, although any person gifted with wisdom would have discernment.

This is the gift of the discerning of spirits. It consists of the ability to discern whether some-thing is of the Holy Spirit or whether it is from an evil spirit. The devil often endeavors to counter-feit the work of the Holy Spirit.

In Acts 11:12 Peter says, "The Spirit told me to have no hesitation about going with them." Here was a very strange circumstance. Peter had just re-ceived a vision, telling him to do something he had never done before. Next he was asked to accom-pany some strange men to go to a place where or-dinarily he would not go. This may have also seemed unwise since this was during the fourth major persecution since Pentecost. But Peter sensed that this was all of the Holy Spirit. He dis-cerned that it was not from the evil one.

When Paul was at Thyatira, a girl began to fol-low his team around the town saying, "These men are servants of the Most High God, who are tell-ing you the way to be saved" (Acts 16:17). Most of us would have said, "Praise the Lord. The people will be persuaded by one of their own. This will establish our testimony in this town."

But Paul said no such thing. He knew that her knowledge was not of the Holy Spirit. So he turned and cast a demon out of her. The situation was of the devil, not of God. My, how the church needs the gift of the discerning of spirits in operation today.

In a church I was pastoring a lady was saved who stuttered so badly that she was able to speak only with the greatest difficulty. One night she was anointed and prayed for. The Lord healed her immediately so that she was able to speak properly. We then asked her to read John 3:16. She immediately went back to stuttering. It was then we realized that she needed more than physical healing. Here was demonic power. Knowing this, we were soon able to bring her to complete deliverance.

About a year later she went back to stuttering. Some people had befriended her and persuaded her differently from that which I had taught her. These people reminded me of Simon the sorcerer in Acts 8 of whom it was said, "This man is the divine power known as the Great Powers" (Acts 8:10). They persuaded her that she once had the "gift of the stammering tongue." Now I had robbed her of that special gift by allowing the devil to bind her.

They had it all backward. In our church there was the gift of the discerning of spirits. In their church they allowed evil spirits to run rampant.

We knew her stammering was not from God. It was definitely from the evil one. After this evil work in her, she was no longer able to witness or pray out loud.

How desperately the church needs this special gift from the Holy Spirit. There is no scriptural exhortation to ask for it, except as may be permitted by the following verse: "And my God will meet all your needs according to his glorious riches in Christ Jesus" (Philippians 4:19). This, of course, would hold with all the gifts. Let us determine what our needs are and then ask.

Tongues. No other gift has been given so much attention in the past century as the gift of tongues. It has been more grossly maligned than any other, both by its opponents and by its proponents. Both sides are extremely guilty.

Right at the start, something needs to be indelibly imprinted upon our minds. Though this fact is seldom mentioned by the commentators, it has been noticed by the many translations since the King James Version of 1611. The Bible nowhere, absolutely nowhere, speaks of "unknown tongues." It speaks of "kinds of tongues," and "diversities of tongues." That is, different kinds of languages.

Pick up your Bible, any translation. Does it say "unknown tongues"? Only in the King James Version is it inserted, supposedly to make for clearer reading and better understanding. But it is not found in the manuscripts. The issue has become the nemesis of the church, based on a word that is not found in the Bible at all. Even some of the commentaries take time to explain what this "unknown" is, devoting space to explain a word that is not there.

When one speaks in tongues, he does not speak an unknown tongue. It is a known tongue. Though it can be, and often is, an unknown tongue to the speaker, it is a tongue that is a real language. It is capable of being understood by another person, even an unsaved person, who knows that particular language.

All the languages indicated in Acts 2 were recognized languages. It is interesting to note that even the local language of Judea was included as another tongue (2:9). Somebody, at least one of the 120, was using his own language, and it is called "tongues." That is because it was used with power to direct people to Christ.

There are a number of words used in the New Testament for tongues. But in Acts and First Corinthians the same word is used with only one exception. This would indicate that the same thing is expected in each book, since there are other words that indicate variations of languages. That one exception is in First Corinthians 14:21 where Paul is quoting from Isaiah 28. That verse indicates a particular language as well, that of Assyria.

Both in Acts 2 and First Corinthians 14, tongues are used as a witness to the unbeliever, not the believer. We all understand Pentecost. Foreign people heard the gospel in their own language. But something very timely is too often missed in First Corinthians 14:22: "Tongues, then, are a sign, not for believers but for unbelievers. . . ." Why is it then, that so many of us insist that tongues are signs for the believers, and are practically never used as a sign to the unsaved?

When tongues were used in a church, anyone who "speaks in a tongue, two—or at the most three—should speak, one at a time, and someone must interpret" (14:27). This refers to the number of people allowed to speak in one service. If Paul had not added, "and at that by course," it might be taken to refer to sentences. But it would be entirely unnecessary for Paul to add that phrase to refer to sentences. That is the only way they can come. It further shows that not more than one person could be speaking at one time. This is grossly overlooked in the misusage of today.

"Someone must interpret," certainly shows that the one using the foreign language was not to do the interpreting. This was part of the safeguard. One person would therefore not be able to fake it all by himself.

It is just as true as it is written, "He who speaks in a tongue edifies himself . . ." (14:4). But nowhere does Paul say that that is what the gift is for. Indeed, he is showing disfavor with the practice. He is trying to show the Corinthians that the gifts are to be used to edify the church. He started off by making this assertion in 12:7 in a sentence and before that by showing they were for ministries to others.

There can be no doubt. Tongues is a true gift of the Holy Spirit for ministries today. The verse that is most often used against this truth is not a verse at all. It is only part of a verse, taken right out of context. The proponents of that view also tell us that prophecy is merely preaching. They say that knowledge is gained by studying. If they were consistent then, their proof text against tongues would read like this, "But where there are prophecies, they will cease; where there are tongues, they will be stilled; where there is knowledge, it will pass away." Obviously, all these things have not happened, if First Corinthians 13:8 is read in its proper context.

However, tongues speaking is sometimes no more than a manifestation of the flesh. In an attempt to appear super-spiritual, some will go to any end to learn this special gift. Many, many people are told that they can be taught to speak in tongues. If that really is the case, then it is the only gift of the Spirit that we have to be taught; all the rest are supernaturally bestowed.

There is also that which comes from the devil, when satan is allowed to take over and actually binds people in his own net. I have seen all three of these being used: the true gift, the flesh and that which is of Satan.

The first is beautiful and is much used of the Lord. The second is distasteful. The last is ugly and used by evil spirits to control, although it may not even appear ugly on the surface.

I want to say a brief word about "the baptism." The term "baptized with the Holy Spirit" (see Matthew 3:11 and Acts 1:5) is never used when referring to an individual. It always refers to a group. The fulfillment on the Day of Pentecost involved a group. Therefore, when an individual talks about "receiving the baptism," he has no scriptural foundation for using the term. It is a misnomer. He may have had an experience, but all religious experiences must be based on the Word of God, or they become suspect.

It is interesting that the gift named by Paul preceding tongues is the gift of the discerning of spirits. I will say it again: We need this gift today. Tongues is now being used almost entirely as a sign that the believer is filled with the Holy Spirit. This is in error. It is contrary to the Scripture. But the false teaching is now going far beyond this. Tongues is also being regarded as a sign that a person is a Christian. Let the saints discern from whence this type of teaching comes.

I have talked to a number of people, including a few pastors, who, as they say, "have unknown tongues." They cannot give me a clear testimony of their salvation. Nor can some of them even give me the plan of salvation when I have asked for it.

I informed a number of pastors that even some cults speak in tongues as part of their religious experience. This only aroused some to say, "Praise the Lord. Then they are saved too."

While ministering in Toronto with Sermons from Science at the Canadian National Exhibition for a number of years, I found a neat little restaurant called Twin Falls. It served exceptionally good steaks at a very reasonable price. It was worth the few extra blocks of travel to go there and sit and relax beside one of the stone walls with the water cascading over the rocks.

One time when I went there I noticed that the sign had been changed. In fact, everything was different about the restaurant, including the waiters to whom I had witnessed many times. As I was ordering my dinner on this particular occasion, the new waiter interrupted me with, "Where did you learn your Greek? It is beautiful. It is also my home dialect."

I immediately grasped the situation. Here was a man far away from home. God had opened his heart to me with the use of a language I had never used before. Now I would be able to give him the gospel in his own dialect, in the language that was so dear to him. One of the interesting things was that I also knew what I was saying. It was as though I were speaking English, but it was coming out in a Greek dialect.

This is tongues. The Bible nowhere indicates that we are to ask for it. He will give it as He wills.

Interpretation. If we can get tongues straightened out in our thinking we will have little problem with this gift. Interpretation involves the translation of the message in tongues into the language that others know. The interpretation may not necessarily be rendered literally. That is why it is called interpretation rather than translation.

Once a pastor tried to show me "a better way." He had a member of my church tape a message in tongues along with an interpretation. Then after it was taped, it was presented to me as proof of what was going on in that pastor's church.

I played the tape many times. In the tongues, there were thirteen repetitions of one statement which sounded like memorized gibberish. There were twelve repetitions of another, and nine of yet another. Seven other phrases were repeated at least three times each.

Then there followed the interpretation. Not once did the interpreter say the same thing twice. Something was definitely wrong. It was a hoax. At the least, a work of the flesh. But when I confronted the pastor, he merely responded that I did not understand interpretation. Perhaps I did not. But I understood him.

There is an interesting rule stated by Paul: "For this reason anyone who speaks in a tongue should pray that he may interpret what he says" (14:13). Here we have a gift that we are told to ask for, on the condition that we speak in tongues as well.

As a young man testified in a church at which I was conducting a weekend of services, it seemed as though the whole congregation arose and started to come forward. Some kneeled down. Some remained standing. Some shouted. This was a little out of my realm since I was accustomed to, "All of these must be done for the strengthening of the church. . . . in a fitting and orderly way"

(14:26, 40). However, since such seemed to be their custom in that church, I asked the pastor to take over, which he did.

With a great deal of care I observed what took place. People groaned, barked, crowed, shouted, spoke out, sang and wept.

After the service I had time with the pastor. I asked the pastor if he spoke in tongues. He did. I asked him if he interpreted. He did not. We talked about, "For this reason anyone who speaks in a tongue should pray that he may interpret what he says," at some length. He had not seen this truth. He just knew that you "put your brain out of gear and coasted into whatever hit you." (My quotation, not his.)

I described to him a certain person who had been at the altar that evening, speaking in tongues.

The pastor knew who I meant—"Oh, yes. He is filled with the Spirit. He is one of my board members." He looked very pleased.

I was not so pleased. "I heard him at the altar," I said. "I heard him cursing God in a foreign language. I knew what he was saying even though it was not English."

"Well," said the pastor, "I knew that he swore at me in English. I did not know that he did it to God in tongues."

"The point is," I said, "you accept this man as Spirit-filled just because he speaks in tongues. But it is not a Holy Spirit tongue. It is an evil tongue from the devil." If the pastor had had the gift of interpretation or even of the discerning of spirits, he would have stopped the whole procedure. As it was he accepted it all as coming from God.

A pastor in Pennsylvania once told me of a message he had given from the pulpit on a Sunday morning in which he spoke in tongues as a demonstration to the congregation of what it was like. He told me that he could not help speaking in tongues. Whenever there came a certain pressure on his tongue, he could not control it. "Oh," said I. "And you think that you are filled with the Holy Spirit? One of the flavors of the fruit of the Spirit is self-control. You should have had control. Further," I continued, "the Scripture tells us, 'The spirits of prophets are subject to the control of the prophets' in First Corinthians 14:32."

He would not listen. Today he is no longer a minister, and the church has been closed. It is just as the Bible says, "if any man be ignorant, let him be ignorant."

We have spent a long time on these gifts. Actually there are a number more found either in First Corinthians 12 or Romans 12. They are all important, but they are not all-important. Our relationship to God is the important thing. Have this relationship in order. Focus on the Giver rather than the gift. God will then be able to do great things through you by giving you the best gifts.

Some gifts are very easily counterfeited or faked. But just try faking wisdom or knowledge or faith. You will not be able to do it for long. We will be known by our fruit. Let us have fruit that remains.

Remember again that these gifts are for Christians. They are not natural abilities that the unsaved can have. They are the abundant enabling of the Holy Spirit for service in the church and through the church. "This is what we speak, not in words taught us by human wisdom but in words taught by the Spirit, expressing spiritual truths in spiritual words. The man without the Spirit does not accept the things [gifts] that come from the Spirit of God, for they are foolishness to him, and he cannot understand them, because they are spiritually discerned" (1 Corinthians 2:13-14).

Gracious Spirit, Holy Ghost,
   Taught by thee, we covet most
Of Thy gifts at Pentecost,
   Holy, heavenly love.

Love is kind and suffers long,
   Love is meek and thinks no wrong,
Love than death itself more strong;
   Therefore, give us love.

Prophecy will fade away,
   Melting in the light of day;
Love will ever with us stay;
   Therefore, give us love.

Faith will vanish into sight;
   Hope be emptied in delight;
Love in heaven will shine more bright;
   Therefore, give us love.

Faith and hope and love we see
   Joining hand in hand agree;
But the greatest of the three,
   And the best is love.

—Christopher Wordsworth

Chapter 12

The Spirit's Gifts to the Churches

The Holy Spirit has special gifts *for* men so men can minister to each other in the churches. Then He has special gifts *of* men so men can minister to the churches.

For example, Scripture says we are given the gift of apostles, not the gift of apostleship. There is a shade of difference. In the gifts of the Holy Spirit to men, the gifts are respected along with the Giver. With the gifts of men to the church, the men are respected along with the Holy Spirit.

The early part of First Corinthians 12 discusses the gifts to men. Then in 12:28 the emphasis changes from the person to the church. In these verses, there can be no mistaking whether one gift is more important than another. The Holy Spirit makes it definite that there is rank among His anointed servants, just as surely as Jesus ranked His disciples. Peter, James and John were in the inner circle with Jesus. And John was the favorite of the three.

Here we are able to see the rankings by the Holy Spirit: "And in the church God has appointed:

first of all apostles,
second prophets,
third teachers;
then workers of miracles,

also those having gifts of healing, those able to help others, those with gifts of administration, and those speaking in different kinds of tongues" (1 Corinthians 12:28).

Then in Ephesians 4:11 he adds, after the prophets and before the teachers, "some to be evangelists, and some to be pastors." We will deal with them in the order they appear in Scripture.

Apostles. Some clichés are picked up unquestioned by the church, whether right or wrong. One cliché that is not found in the Bible is "the apostolic age." This is used to define a specific time in the history of the church. It is used mainly by ultra or hyper-dispensationalists, who maintain that everything changed when that period or age was over. As a rule they eliminate miracles, healings, tongues, etc., as viable tools in the church today.

People of this persuasion usually agree that the gift of apostleship ceased with the death of the Twelve. They use such verses as, "God has put us apostles on display at the end of the procession . . ." (1 Corinthians 4:9). They say that "end" should be before "apostles." But not so. Paul is using the Roman method of parading criminals as an illustration. In these parades, they put the prisoners on the last floats. If the prisoner was to be set free, the float was highly perfumed and gave off a sweet aroma. If the man was to be put to death the odour was offensive as we see in Second Corinthians 2:16: "To the one we are the smell of death; to the other, the fragrance of life."

Early in my ministry I prepared a study proving that there were to be only twelve apostles, no more and no less. Further, I preached that the gift of apostleship was no longer in the church. I received many favorable comments on my message. But I have never used it since that very first time. I cannot.

All my arguments have evaporated in the light of God's Word. I have had to do an about-face. I had insisted that the upper room election was ill-timed, and Matthias was numbered with the eleven by the eleven, but not by God. God was going to choose Paul, but he was not saved yet.

But then I discovered that this did not give me room in my philosophy for Barnabas who is called an apostle in Acts 14:14. The James of Acts 12:17 is the Lord's earthly brother and not the brother of John. John's brother, James, had already been killed by Herod (Acts 12:2). The James of Acts 12:17 is the chairman of the apostles—hardly a fitting position if he were not an apostle himself.

And what can we say about Andronicus and Junias who were eminent apostles among the apostles (Romans 16:7)? The latter use of *apostles* does not necessarily mean The Twelve, but likely refers to a number of other apostles among the Romans.

Apollos is not directly designated as an apostle. But who would deny him this place after reading about the prominence that Paul gave Him in First Corinthians 1:12; 3:4; 4:6; 16:12; and Titus 3:4? Paul places him right between himself and Peter.

In Second Corinthians 8:23, Titus is called an apostle of the church, the term used being *apostoloi*, and not the more general term for messenger, *angelos*. And if Titus was an apostle, then surely Timothy must have been one as well. The same holds with Epaphroditus in Philippians 2:25. He is Paul's "brother, fellow worker and fellow soldier, who is also your messenger (*apostoloi*)."

And all this besides "first, Simon (who is called Peter) and his brother Andrew; James son of Zebedee, and his brother John; Philip and Bartholomew; Thomas and Matthew the tax collector; James son of Alphaeus, and Thaddaeus; Simon the Zealot and Judas Iscariot, who betrayed him" (Matthew 10:2-4).

These apostles were people who laid the foundation. It is obvious that they had many gifts of the Spirit, if the ones whose works we know are any measure of the rest. They were the ones who were so gifted that they could begin churches by laying the firm foundation, and still be able to oversee large territories besides. They had to have great gifts of wisdom, knowledge and faith, and many of the other gifts as well.

These men are not lacking today. I have seen them at work, and their work remains. Many readers will recognize the name of Gordon A. Skitch. It is estimated that he started more churches in Canada as an evangelist, pastor and administrator than any other person. He even took a little time out to be one of the co-founders of the Canadian Bible College from which has developed the Canadian Theological Seminary. And there are a host like him, some gone and some still with us.

The things some have said are the qualifications for apostleship are mere inference. Though it did happen to some of the apostles in Scripture, seeing and feeling the Lord physically was not a prerequisite for apostleship.

Paul said, "I laid a foundation . . ." (1 Corinthians 3:10). This seems to be the better qualification. ". . . built on the foundation of the apostles and prophets, with Christ Jesus himself as the chief cornerstone" (Ephesians 2:20).

But one might argue, "Then are we to build upon the foundation of Jesus or the apostles?" The answer is "both." And after all we are to "fix your thoughts on Jesus, the apostle and high priest whom we confess" (Hebrews 3:1). Jesus Christ, also, was an apostle.

Prophets. As it is difficult to see the whole aspect of apostleship, so it is difficult for us to see the work of the prophets in today's church. This is mostly because we have changed our terminology.

The prophet of the New Testament writings would compare to the evangelist of today. But, alas, many men and women are termed evangelists who are not prophets, nor do they have the gifts that a prophet of God needs. They may travel from church to church, but they are not evangelists or prophets in the biblical sense of the words.

The task of a prophet is sometimes to *foretell*. As in Acts 21:10-11, where Agabus showed Paul what would happen to him if he went to Jerusalem. But in both the Old Testament and the New, the great work of the prophet was to *forthtell* the message with power and authority. It is also a ministry of exhortation as we see in Acts 15:32, "Judas and Silas, who themselves were prophets, said much to encourage and strengthen the brothers."

Prophets are also foundation builders like the apostles. It ought to be part of the work of evangelists to plant new churches, teach the people for a time and then leave a pastor to shepherd the new flock. This is one of the New Testament methods.

Evangelists. Having shown that a prophet really corresponds to the evangelist in today's church, what is there left for the biblical evangelist to do? A biblical evangelist is none other than our modern missionary.

The evangelist is a rare breed in the New Testament with only two illustrations. Philip is called an evangelist in Acts 21:8. He is the one who led the Ethiopian eunuch to the Lord. This ignited a mighty missionary movement to the core of Africa. Timothy is told to do the work of an evangelist in Second Timothy 4:5, but we are not told specifically what this work was.

Why were there so few of these missionaries in the New Testament? Well, there were many, but they are called by their higher ranking. For example, Thomas, as most Christians know, even took the gospel to India. He is called an apostle in Scripture, but he was also a missionary.

Now let us review. The apostles are apostles. The prophets are today's evangelists. The evangelists are today's missionaries. Some of the versions even dare to say so.

Pastors. A pastor is literally a shepherd. It was the task of the pastor to "Be shepherds of God's flock that is under your care, serving as overseers . . ." (1 Peter 5:2). In Paul's farewell message to the Ephesians, he told the pastor-elders that "after I leave, savage wolves will come in among you and will not spare the flock. . . . So be on your guard!" (Acts 20:29-31).

Since the pastor, because of his position, must teach the flock as well as protect it, the Holy Spirit links the two gifts of pastoring and teaching together, making the pastor really a pastor-teacher. Paul wrote to Timothy that the pastor must be "able to teach" (1 Timothy 3:2).

However, the two are only partially linked. Ephesians 4:11 says that He gave some churches apostles. He gave some churches evangelists. He gave some churches missionaries. And He gave some churches pastors and teachers. The *and* definitely separates the two, indicating that they may be different men. The *some* connects them to show that the two gifts may be in the one man.

I have checked every Greek text available to me. The *and* is very definitely there, even though many commentators would like to replace it by using a hyphen. Thus the designation pastor-teacher is not found in the Scripture, even though it may suggest a proper way to exercise these gifts in the church in many instances.

Teachers. Most of this has already been explained. However, it should be remembered that God does have specially gifted people for the ministry of teaching in the churches. This can even be enlarged since the gift of teaching goes well beyond the confines of the church itself. This is the special enduement whereby a person is equipped by the Holy Spirit to instruct others.

With such a gift available, Christian teachers ought to be the best teachers in the world. Many times they are not the best teachers. It is a gift that is neglected. If it were not neglected, what a great testimony teachers would have in society today.

If the church of Jesus Christ would mature sufficiently to see that God has given her these gifted men we have discussed in this chapter, what a change there would be in some circles. But the church fails to appreciate God's gifts. People get disgruntled. They oppose the man that God sent them. He was God's gift to them, and they reject His gift. Most of the time the man is even one the church chose for herself after he had candidated.

Murmuring is a sin. How often judgment was brought in the Old Testament to the people who murmured against God and Moses, or against Moses and Aaron. It is no different today except for the type of judgment that is being meted out.

While apostles, evangelists, missionaries, pastors and teachers are given "to prepare God's people for works of service, so that the body of Christ may be built up" (Ephesians 4:12), there is much that we can become without having all the types of gifted men to assist us to grow in the Lord. Let us pray the following prayer for ourselves:

Spirit of God, descend upon my heart;
    Wean it from earth, through all its
        pulses move;
Stoop to my weakness, mighty as Thou art,
    And make me love Thee as I ought
        to love.

I ask no dream, no prophetic ecstasies,
    No sudden rending of the veil of clay,
No angelic visitant, no opening skies;
    But take the dimness of my soul away.

Teach me to feel that Thou art always nigh;
    Teach me the struggles of the soul
        to bear,
To check the rising doubt, the rebel sigh;
    Teach me the patience of
        unanswered prayer.

Teach me to love Thee as Thine angels love,
   One holy passion filling all my frame;
The baptism of the heaven-descended Dove;
   My heart an altar, and Thy love
      the flame.

—George Croly

Chapter 13

The Holy Spirit and Prayer

For this final chapter I want to return to the last sentence in the Bible that mentions the three persons of the Trinity by name, Jude 20-21: "But you, dear friends, build yourselves up in your most holy faith and pray in the Holy Spirit. Keep yourselves in God's love as you wait for the mercy of our Lord Jesus Christ to bring you to eternal life."

What is praying in the Holy Spirit? Can it be praying in tongues, when a person prays in a language that he does not understand? What does praying in the Holy Spirit involve?

Paul gives us a little insight in Romans 8:14-15: "Because those who are led by the Spirit of God are sons of God. . . . You received the Spirit of sonship. And by him we cry, '*Abba*, Father.' " Praying in the Spirit involves being led by the Spirit, so that the Holy Spirit in us prays through us.

A companion verse credits the cry of "*Abba*, Father" to the Holy Spirit: "Because you are sons,

God sent the Spirit of his Son into our hearts, the Spirit who calls out, '*Abba*, Father' " (Galatians 4:6).

One of these verses ascribes the cry of "Abba, Father" to us. The other attributes it to the Holy Spirit. A contradiction? No. Both are true. We cry out, but the Holy Spirit is crying through us.

Paul further says that we are to be "faithful in prayer" (Romans 12:12). We are to "pray continually" (1 Thessalonians 5:17).

As we mature in Christ there is a danger that we may think we can get along without prayer. But we cannot. Without prayer the Holy Spirit will not work through us. Without Him working through us, our work is just so much "wood, hay or straw, . . . It will be revealed with fire, and the fire will test the quality of each man's work" (1 Corinthians 3:12-13).

The art of prayer requires fervency, perseverance, love, the gift of faith and boldness tempered with humility. With this there will be the outpouring of ecstatic prayer as the Holy Spirit anoints us and speaks through us. Paul put it this way in Ephesians 6:18: "Pray in the Spirit on all occasions with all kinds of prayers and requests. With this in mind, be alert and always keep on praying for all the saints."

In Romans 8:26-27 we are told: "In the same way, the Spirit helps us in our weakness. We do not know what we ought to pray for, but the Spirit himself intercedes for us with groans that words cannot express. And he who searches our hearts knows the mind of the Spirit, because the Spirit intercedes for the saints in accordance with God's will."

This is the deepest praying. No. It is not, as some have said, praying in an unknown tongue. This is prayer that cannot be uttered, not prayer that is uttered. It is the Spirit praying through us when we are inarticulate. We have control, but we do not know what to say. Remember one of the keys? "The spirits of prophets are subject to the control of prophets" (1 Corinthians 14:32).

We have so much about the Holy Spirit and prayer in the Bible. How is it, then, that we neglect Him in our praying? A candid observation reveals that an older saint generally prays to the Father. A younger Christian usually prays to Jesus, the Son. Each one forgets the Holy Spirit. This is extreme.

Of course it is just as extreme to pray to the Holy Spirit only, as some are prone to do. That is extremism in the opposite direction. Almost always the pendulum swings too far. Perhaps we could come back to the middle and recognize the Holy Spirit in our praying, along with the Father and the Son.

It appears that the early disciples were so accustomed to speaking to the Holy Spirit that Ananias and Sapphira even lied to Him: "Then Peter said, 'Ananias, how is it that Satan has so filled your heart that you have lied to the Holy Spirit? . . . You have not lied to men but to God'" (Acts 5:3-4).

(Note: If any reader still has a question about the Holy Spirit being a person and being God, this passage should remove all doubt.)

In the benediction often used to close worship services, we are exhorted to have communion with the Holy Spirit: "May the grace of the Lord Jesus Christ, and the love of God, and the fellowship of the Holy Spirit be with you all " (2 Corinthians 13:14). It is unlikely that we will have much communion if we do not have conversation. After all, He is God, and we all talk to God. But should we address only two-thirds of the Godhead? I think not.

We often regard the hymn writers as great men of faith. Think of them: Isaac Watts, Martin Luther, John and Charles Wesley, John Newton, A.B. Simpson, Oswald J. Smith, Fanny Crosby, Philip P. Bliss, Frances Havergal and a host of others.

Have you ever noticed that when these hymn writers wrote about the Holy Spirit, the hymns were often prayers? That is right. They prayed directly to the Holy Spirit. There was sweet communion there.

Pick up almost any hymnal and turn to the section on God the Holy Spirit. Almost all the hymns are prayers directed in their entirety to the Holy Spirit. Are we missing something?

If you have read the prayer hymns quoted in this book, you have already started down the path to balance in prayer. You have been recognizing the Holy Spirit in your praying. Look back over them again. Are they not all prayers directed to the Holy Spirit?—not the Father nor the Son? Did you pray the hymns as you read them? Were you praying as you sang some of these hymns many times through the years?

Let us pray one more of these wonderful hymns in which the writer addresses the Holy Spirit:

Holy Spirit, faithful Guide,
    Ever near the Christian's side,
Gently lead us by the hand—
    Pilgrims in a desert land.
Weary souls fore'er rejoice,
    While they hear that sweetest voice,
Whispering softly, "Wanderer, come,
    Follow Me, I'll guide thee home."

Ever present, truest Friend,
    Ever near Thine aid to lend,
Leave us not to doubt and fear,
    Groping on in darkness drear.
When the storms are raging sore,
    Hearts grow faint, and hopes give o'er;
Whispering softly, "Wanderer, come,
    Follow Me, I'll guide thee home."

When our days of toil shall cease,
    Waiting still for sweet release,
Nothing left but heaven and prayer,
    Wondering if our names are there;
Wading deep and dismal flood,
    Pleading nought but Jesus' blood,

Whispering softly, "Wanderer, come,
Follow me, I'll guide thee home."

—Marcus M. Wells

Epilogue

The purpose of this book has been to teach the reader about the Holy Spirit, who He is and what He does. But it is also the hope of the author that it will bring people into a closer relationship with the Lord Jesus Christ. The greatest ministry of the Holy Spirit is to exalt the Savior.

The following testimony of Dr. A.B. Simpson has become my testimony and desire. May it become yours as well, as together we "press on toward the goal to win the prize for which God has called me heavenward in Christ Jesus" (Philippians 3:14).

> O souls that are seeking for pleasure,
>   Your follies and pleasures pursue;
> Contend for the prizes of fortune,
>   Such trifles may answer for you.
> But mine is a nobler ambition;
>   I seek for a richer reward;
> I want to be Christlike and holy;
>   I want to be just like my Lord.
>
> I'm weary of sinning and stumbling,
>   Repenting and falling again;

I'm tired of resolving and striving,
   And finding the struggle so vain.
I long for an arm to uphold me,
   A will that is stronger than mine;
A Saviour to cleanse me and fill me,
   And keep me by power divine.

I want to be patient and gentle,
   Long-suffering and loving and kind,
As quick to acknowledge my failings
   As I to another's am blind.
I want to be quiet and peaceful,
   Though tempests around me may roll.
The stillness of Jesus within me,
   Possessing and filling my soul.

I long, oh, I long to be holy,
   Conformed to His will and His Word;
I want to be gentle and Christlike,
   I want to be just like my Lord.

—A.B. Simpson

---

1 Corinthians 14

The many problems that have arisen through centuries of discussion concerning the ministry of the Holy Spirit are the results of two things. The first is the result of lack of knowledge, when the Christian fails to read and study God's Word. The second comes from misinterpretation.

Misinterpretation, also, can be divided into two areas of study. The first has to do with mindset. This is often created when young people especially, but older people as well, hear the same thing repeatedly, over a period of time, and accept it, whether right or wrong.

The second area cannot be blamed on anybody else or anything else, only ourselves. It comes about when we are not "rightly dividing the word of truth" (2 Timothy 2:15, KJV). We know that we must not make any verse stand by itself. We must compare Scripture with Scripture, and do so within the context. But, so often, the Christian fails to follow the rules in Bible study, even though they follow the rules in other walks of life.

Immediately after my original book on the Holy Spirit was published, I was asked to speak at St. Paul Bible College, now called Crown College. I was to bring enough copies of the book for each person at the college. And I should be prepared to speak morning and evening, with the ministry of the Holy Spirit as the central theme.

I interpreted the request inaccurately. I thought I was going to be the speaker at their annual Spiritual Emphasis Week. It was at the usual time of the year, and the theme was on the deeper life. But I was mistaken. They had already experienced Spiritual Emphasis Week, and it was a minor disaster—a major failure.

It seems that twenty freshmen had enrolled, not to study to show themselves approved unto God, but rather to "straighten out the college" on its theology regarding the Holy Spirit.

During that period of time, as I traveled across the United States and Canada, I found this type of thing happening repeatedly. Young people would respond to an altar call, not for help, but rather to help the counselor. Whenever this happened, the people would be faced with their own problem of deception, often to their chagrin.

I arrived at the college without knowing the background of events. And I need not to have been advised. Speakers often have more liberty to speak when they do not know the problems.

Sometimes when they know the problems, they make the problems even larger. However, I was informed that students were not expected to miss classes while the meetings were in progress, unless for private consultation.

So it was that I arranged for students who had problems to meet me privately. They would fill out a 3 x 5 filing card, receive a time slot, and the administration would be informed of the schedule.

I was amazed at the response. I found it necessary to counsel all day long except for the actual service times. There were even counseling sessions as we ate breakfast, lunch and dinner. It was a very full week.

Generally, when students came into my temporary office, knowing they had a set period of time, they would start telling their problems immediately after I led in prayer. But then it happened. After a short prayer, a student merely sat there looking at me, almost daring me to open my mouth. Which I did. "What need do you have today?"

"And what need do you have today?" came the student's response. I was not taken by surprise. "I understand that you have signed a card indicating that you have a need, and you have used this system to come to help me in my spiritual life. Is that correct?" It was.

"Well, it is rather interesting young man, that God would send me from another country to help students like you, and then we end up in the same room with you going to help me. To do what I am doing has been arranged ethically. To do what you are doing has been arranged through deception. Do you know who the great deceiver is?"

He avoided the question with, "What right do you have to talk to me like that when you don't speak in tongues?"

"Now we have an additional problem," I responded. "You have accused me of not being Spirit-filled because I do not speak in tongues, and you don't know whether I speak in tongues or not. That is being judgmental to add to your sin of deception."

After talking to him briefly, a plan began to formulate in my mind. It was obvious he was not skilled in the topic he was proffering. And I wanted him to be. I asked him if he would be honest enough to do an experiment with me. Would he do an assignment and bring it back to me no later than Thursday night? And would he keep the assignment secret until after he brought it back to me? He replied in the affirmative.

This happened twenty times during the week. I wondered how successful this assignment would be. Since then I have given it to people privately hundreds of times, and put it in lectures dozens of times.

By Thursday night sixteen of the twenty had come back with their homework, either complete or nearly so. And all sixteen told me they had been wrong, and humbly asked what they needed to do next. They had not come to study. They had come to correct. Some had even quit jobs to do so.

I replied, "The devil sent you here to stir up trouble. But God allowed this to happen so you could come here to learn the truth. I challenge you to stay and learn for at least this semester. But there is something you will have to do. Tomorrow morning in chapel, I will give you opportunity to stand up, confess your pride and ask forgiveness for the disturbances you have caused." All sixteen did so.

It is a very simple assignment, although time consuming. You will need a number of sheets of 8½ x 11 lined paper. Since you will want to keep your work, you will want to have a binder as well.

The pages shall be divided vertically into four section, with the sections entitled Vs, Text, Interpretation and Corrections. Under Vs you will simply put the verse number from First Corinthians 14. Then under the Text heading you will print out the entire verse from the Bible. Use any translation you like, but once having chosen the translation do not change.

Then in the third column, print what you think that verse actually means. Let it stand by itself, because that is how most people use First Corinthians 14. Do not worry about any contradictions in your interpretation. Finish the entire chapter.

After you have finished the entire chapter, read your interpretation through a number of times. You will likely notice that you have contradicted yourself a number of times. Then print in the fourth column your reconciliation. "X-out" where you were wrong in your former analysis in column three, and use column four as your final product. You may be thoroughly surprised.

In all of this, you should remember that almost the entire book of First Corinthians is given for correction. The Holy Spirit is correcting all the things that were wrong in the church. Oddly enough, when the writer, Paul, makes a statement to say what they were doing, the reader often takes that to be an example of what we should do. In fact, he states that this is what they did, and now this is what they should have done.

You will have the best commentary there is on First Corinthians 14. And it will be your very own. And it likely will be better than anything either you or I have read in the writings of some great scholars. But only *you* can do it!

Here is an example to get you started:

1 Corinthians 14

Vs	Bible Text	My Interpretation	My Correction
3	But one who prophesies speaks to men for edification, and . . .	~~Prophecy is a gift whereby the speaker brings others so Christ.~~	There must be a difference between prophecy and preaching . . .
22	. . . but prophecy is for a sign, not to unbelievers, but to those who believe	Prophecy is a gift whereby Christians receive direction	

SCRIPTURE INDEX

Revelation

Index of Hymns

Bibliography

Allan, Roland. *The Ministry of the Holy Spirit.* Ed. by David M. Paton. Grand Rapids, MI: William B. Eerdmans Publishing Company, 1960.

Augsburger, Myron S. *Quench Not the Spirit.* Scottsdale, PA: Herald Press, 1961.

Bale, Milton M. *Types of the Holy Spirit.* New York: The Alliance Press Company, n.d.

Barclay, William. *The Promise of the Spirit.* Philadelphia, PA: Westminster Press, 1960.

Barret, Charles Kingsley. *The Holy Spirit and the Gospel Tradition.* London: S.P.C.K., 1966.

Berkhof, Hendricker. *The Doctrine of the Holy Spirit.* Richmond, VA: John Knox Press, 1964.

Bickersteth, Edward Henry. *The Holy Spirit, His Person and Work.* Grand Rapids, MI: Kregel Publishers, 1959.

Biederwolf, William Edward. *A Help to the Study of the Holy Spirit.* Toronto: Fleming H. Revell Company, 1903.

Blackwood, Andrew W. *The Holy Spirit in Your Life.* Grand Rapids, MI: Baker Publishing House, 1957.

Boer, Harry R. *Pentecost and Missions.* Grand Rapids, MI: William B. Eerdmans Publishing Company, 1961.

Boice, James Montgomery. *Awakening to God.* Downers Grove, IL: InterVarsity Press, 1979.

Bosworth, F.F. *Do All Speak with Tongues?* Dayton, OH: Dayton Publishing Company, 1934.

Broomall, Wick. *The Holy Spirit.* Grand Rapids, MI: Baker Publishing House, 1963.

Brown, Dale W. *Flamed by the Spirit.* Elgin, IL: Brethren Press, 1978.

Brown, W. Herbert. *Fire, Radiance and Love.* Wheaton, IL: Tyndale House Publishers, 1979.

Brownville, Charles Gordon. *Symbols of the Holy Spirit.* Wheaton, IL: Tyndale House Publishers, 1978.

Brunk, George R. II. *Encounter with the Holy Spirit.* Scottsdale, PA: Herald Press, 1972.

Cale, Norman McLeod. *The Vintage.* London: Religious Tract Society, n.d.

Campbell, Bob. *The Baptism in the Holy Spirit.* Monroeville: PA: Whitaker House, 1973.

Campus Crusade for Christ International. *How to Experience and Share the Abundant Christian Life.* San Bernardino, CA: Campus Crusade, 1971.

Candlish, James S. *The Work of the Holy Spirit.* Edinburgh: Clark, n.d.

Carter, Charles Webb. *The Person and Ministry of the Holy Spirit.* Grand Rapids, MI: Baker Book House, 1974.

Chadwick, Samuel. *The Way to Pentecost.* London: Hodder and Stoughton, n.d.

Chafer, Lewis Sperry. *He That Is Spiritual.* Findlay, OH: Dunham Publishing Company, 1918.

Chapman, J.B. *Holiness Triumphant.* Kansas City, MO: Beacon Hill Press, 1946.

Christian, An Unknown. *How to Live the Victorious Life*. Grand Rapids, MI: Zondervan Publishing House, 1966.

Conner, Walter Thomas. *The Work of the Holy Spirit*. Nashville, TN: Broadman Press, n.d.

Crammer, Raymond L. *The Master Key*. Los Angeles, CA: Cowan, 1951.

Criswell, Wallie A. *The Holy Spirit in Today's World*. Grand Rapids, MI: Zondervan Publishing House, 1966.

Damboriena, Prudencio. *Tongues as of Fire*. Washington, DC: Corpus Books, n.d.

David, George T.B. *When the Fire Fell*. Philadelphia, PA: Millions Testament League, 1945.

DiGangi, Mariano. *The Spirit of Christ*. Grand Rapids, MI: Baker Book House, 1975.

Dillistone, F.W. *The Holy Spirit in Life Today*. London: Canterbury, 1946.

Doing, Robert Burns. *Three Who Dance Together*. Waco, TX: Word Books, 1970.

Doleman, D.H. *Simple Talks on the Holy Spirit*. London: Marshall, Morgan and Scott, n.d.

Douty, Norman F. *Filled with the Spirit*. Findlay, OH: Fundamental Truth Publishers, n.d.

Duncan, Homer. *Revival Fires*. Bubbock: Missionary Crusader, n.d.

Dunn, James. *Jesus and the Spirit*. London: S.C.M. Press, 1975.

Duscher, John M. *Spirit Fruit*. Scottsdale, PA: Herald Press, 1974.

Erdman, Charles R. *The Spirit and Christ*. New York, NY: Doran, 1926.

Ervin, Howard M. *These Are Not Drunken as Ye Suppose.* Plainfield, NJ: Logos International, 1968.

Evans, Louise H. *Life's Hidden Power.* Westwood. NJ: Fleming H. Revell Company, 1958.

Fife, Eric S. *The Holy Spirit.* Grand Rapids, MI: Zondervan Publishing House, 1978.

Finney, Charles G. *Lectures on Revivals of Religion.* London: Milner, 1888.

Fitch, William. *The Ministry of the Holy Spirit.* Grand Rapids, MI: Zondervan Publishing House, 1974.

Foster, K. Neill. *The Discerning Christian.* Harrisburg, PA: Christian Publications, Inc., 1981.

——*The Happen Stance.* Beaverlodge: Horizon House, 1977.

——*Help! I Believe in Tongues.* 1975.

——*A Revolution of Love.* Minneapolis, MN: Dimension Books, 1973.

Francis, Mabel R. *Filled With the Spirit....Then What?* Harrisburg: Christian Publications, Inc., 1974.

Frodsham, Stanley Howard. *The Spirit-Filled Life.* Grand Rapids, MI: Eerdmans Pubishing Co., 1948.

Frost, Henry W. *Who Is the Holy Spirit?* London: Fleming H. Revell Co., 1938.

Frost, Robert C. *Aglow with the Spirit.* Rev. Ed. Plainfield, NJ: Logos International, 1971.

——*The Biology of the Holy Spirit.* Old Tappan, NJ: Fleming H. Revell Co., 1975.

——*The Overcoming Life.* Plainfield, NJ: Logos, Intermational, 1971.

——*Set My Spirit Free.* 1973.

Gardiner, F. Stuart. *The Power of the Spirit and the Needs of the Church.* Edinburgh: Clark, 1926.

Gee, Donald. *Concerning Spiritual Gifts.* Springfield, MO: Gospel Publishing House, n.d.

Gesswein, Armin. *With One Accord in One Place.* Harrisburg, PA: Christian Publications, Inc., 1978.

Gillquist, Peter E. *Let's Quit Fighting About the Holy Spirit.* Grand Rapids, MI: Zondervan Publishing House, 1974.

Gordon, Adonirom Judson. *The Holy Spirit in Missions.* New York, NY: Fleming H. Revell Co., 1893.

——*The Ministry of the Spirit.* 1894.

Gore, Charles. *The Holy Spirit and the Church.* New York, NY: Scribner, 1924.

Graham, Billy (William Franklin). *The Holy Spirit.* Waco, TX: Word Books, 1978.

Green, Edward Michael Bankers. *I Believe in the Holy Spirit.* Grand Rapids, MI: Eerdmans Publishing House, 1975.

Greenfield, John. *Why the Spirit Came.* Minneapolis, MN: Bethany Fellowship, 1967.

Grenkel, Hermann. *The Influence of the Holy Spirit.* Philadelphia, PA: Fortress Press, 1979.

Hammond, T.C. *In Understanding Be Men.* London: Inter-Varsity Fellowship, 1936.

Harris, Evan R. *Receive Ye the Holy Spirit.* London: Marshall, Morgan and Scott, n.d.

Henderlite, Rachel. *The Holy Spirit in Christian Education.* Philadelphia, PA: Westminster Press, 1964.

Hendley, George Stuart. *Theology of Nature.* Philadelphia, PA: Westminster, 1980.

Hoffman, Jasper Adam. *Upper Room Messages.* Butler, IN: Hingley Press, n.d.

Hochema, Anthony A. *Holy Spirit Baptism.* Grand Rapids, MI: Eerdmans Publishing House, 1972.

Holdcroft, L. Thomas. *The Holy Spirit.* Springfield, MO: Gospel Publishing House, 1979.

Horton, Harold. *The Gifts of the Spirit.* London: Assemblies of God, 1934.

Howard, David M. *By the Power of the Holy Spirit.* Downers Grove, IL: InterVarsity Press, 1973.

Hucheson, Richard G. *Wheel Within a Wheel.* Atlanta, GA: John Knox Press, 1973.

Hummel, Charles E. *Fire in the Fireplace: Contemporary Charismatic Renewal.* Downers Grove, IL: InterVarsity Press, 1978.

Hunt, Garth. *God is Not Hiding.* Harrisburg, PA: Christian Publications, Inc., 1973.

Ironside, Harry A. *Praying in the Holy Ghost.* New York, NY: Loizeaux Brothers, 1946.

James, Maynard G. *I Believe in the Holy Spirit.* Minneapolis, MN: Bethany Fellowship, 1965.

Johnston, George. *The Spirit-Paraclete in the Gospel of John.* Cambridge: Union Press. 1970.

Kelly, W. *Lectures on the New Testament Doctrine of the Holy Spirit.* London: Broom and Rouse, 1867.

King, William P., ed. *After Pentecost, What?* Nashville, TN: Cokesbury Press, 1930.

——*Sermons of Power.* 1930.

Kinghorn, Kenneth Gavin. *Fresh Wind of the Spirit*. Nashville. TN: Abingdon Press, 1975.

Kirkpatrick, Dow, ed. *The Holy Spirit*. Nashville, TN: Tidings Press, 1974.

Koch, Kurt. *The Revival in Indonesia*. Grand Rapids, MI: Kregel Publications, n.d.

Kraus, Clyde Norman. *The Community of the Spirit*. Grand Rapids, MI: Eerdmans Publishing House, 1974.

Kung, Hans and Moltmann, Jurgen, eds. *Conflicts About the Holy Spirit*. New York, NY: Seabury Press, 1979.

Kuyper, Abraham. *The Work of the Holy Spirit*. Grand Rapids, MI: Eerdmans Publishing House, 1900.

LaHaye, Tim. *Spirit-Controlled Temperament*. Wheaton, IL: Tyndale House Publishers, 1966.

Lehman, Chester Kindig. *The Holy Spirit and the Holy Life*. Scottsdale, PA: Herald Press, 1959.

Lockyer, Herbert. *All the Divine Names and Titles in the Bible*. Grand Rapids, MI: Zondervan Publishing House, 1975.

Logdson, S. Franklin. *The Holy Spirit at Work*. Chicago, IL: Moody Press, 1960.

——-*The Lord of the Harvest*. Grand Rapids, MI: Zondervan Publishing House, 1954.

Lutzer, Erwin W. *Flames of Freedom*. Chicago, IL: Moody Press, 1967.

Macdonald, A.J. *The Interpreter Spirit*. London: S.P.C.K., 1944.

MacNeil, John, *The Spirit-Filled Life*. Chicago, IL: Moody Colportage Association, 1896.

MacPherson, Ian. *Like a Dove Descending*. Minneapolis, MN: Bethany Fellowship, 1969.

Madsen, Paul O. *When the Spirit is Lord.* Pant Nagar, Bombay: Gospel Literature Service, 1970.

Marsh, F.E. *Emblems of the Holy Spirit.* Grand Rapids, MI: Kregel Publications, 1957.

Marshall, Catherine Wood. *The Helper.* Waco, TX: Word Books, 1978.

McConkey, James H. *The Three-fold Secret of the Holy Spirit.* Pittsburgh. PA: Silver Publishing Company. 1920.

McCrossan, T.J. *Christ's Paralysed Church X-Rayed.* Seattle, WA: T.J. McCrossan, 1937.

McLeish, Alexander. *The Priority of the Holy Spirit in Christian Witness.* London: World Dominion Press, 1961.

Metcalfe, J.C. *The Bible and the Spirit-Filled Life.* Poole: Overcomer Literature Trust, n.d.

Meyers, Cortland. *The Real Holy Spirit.* New York, NY: Fleming H. Revell Co., 1909.

Miles, F.J. *The Greatest Unseen Power in the World.* Minneapolis, MN: Wilson Press, 1944.

Moody, Dwight L. *Secret Power.* New York, NY: Fleming H. Revell Co., 1881.

Morgan, G. Campbell. *The Spirit of God.* Westwood, NJ: Fleming H. Revell Co., 1953.

Morison, James. *St. Paul's Teaching on Sanctification.* London: Hodder and Stoughton, 1886.

Morris, Leon. *The Spirit of the Living God.* London: InterVarsity Press, 1960.

Moule, Charles Francis Digby. The Holy Spirit. Grand Rapids, MI: Eerdmans Publishing Company, 1979.

Moule, Handley Care Glyn. *The Person and Work of the Holy Spirit*. Grand Rapids, MI: Kregel Publications 1977.

Murray, Andrew. *The Full Blessing of Pentecost*. Toronto: Fleming H. Revell Co., 1908.

——*The Master's Indwelling*. Minneapolis, MN: Bethany Fellowship, Inc., 1977.

——*The Power of the Spirit*. London: James Nesbet and Co., 1896.

——*The Spirit of Christ*.

Nee, Watchman (To-Sheng). *The Release of the Spirit*. Hong Kong: Sure Foundation, 1965.

Neve, Lloyd. *The Spirit of God in the Old Testament*. Tokyo: Seibunsha, 1972.

Newberry William Wisdom. *Untangling Live Wires*. Seattle, WA: Voice of Deeper Truth, 1945.

Oates, Wayne Edward. *The Holy Spirit in Five Worlds*. New York, NY: Association Press, 1968.

Ockenga, Harold John. *Power Through Pentecost*. Grand Rapids, MI: Wm. B. Eerdmans, 1959.

——*The Spirit of the Living God*. New York, NY: Fleming H. Revell Co., 1947.

Opsahl, Paul D., ed. *The Holy Spirit in the Life of the Church*. Minneapolis, MN: Augsburg Publishing House, 1978.

Owen, John. *The Holy Spirit*. Grand Rapids, MI: Kregel Publications, 1954.

Pasche, Rene. *The Person and Work of the Holy Spirit*. Chicago, IL: Moody Press, 1954.

Palmer, Edwin H. *The Holy Spirit*. Rev. ed. Philadelphia, PA: Presbyterian and Reformed Press, 1964.

Paxson, Ruth. *Rivers of Living Water*. Chicago, IL: Moody Press, 1941.

Penn-Lewis, Jesse. *Soul and Spirit*. Bournemough: Overcomer Book Room, n.d.

Rahmer, Karl, *The Spirit in the Church*. New York, NY: Seabury Press, 1979

Ramm, Bernard L. *Rapping About the Spirit*. Waco, TX: Word Books, 1974.

——*The Witness of the Spirit*. Grand Rapids, MI: Eerdmans Publishing House, 1960.

Ramsey, Arthur Michael. *Come Holy Spirit*. New York, NY: Morehouse-Barlow Co., 1976

——*The Holy Spirit*. Grand Rapids, MI: Eerdmans Publishing House.

Rasmussen, A.W. *The Last Chapter*. Monroeville, PA: Banner Publishing, 1973.

Rice, John R. *The Power of Pentecost* Wheaton, IL: Sword of the Lord Publishers, 1949.

——*The Soul-Winners Fire*. 1941.

Richards, Lang. *Becoming One in the Spirit*. Wheaton, IL: Victor Books, 1973.

Robinson, Henry Wheeler. *The Christian Experience of the Holy Spirit*. New York, NY: Harper Brothers.

Russel, Walter. *The Burning Bush*. Toronto: Henderson and Co., 1902.

Ryrie, Charles Caldwell. *The Holy Spirit*. Chicago, IL: Moody Press., 1965.

Sanders, John Oswald. *The Holy Spirit and His Gifts. Rev.* ed. Grand Rapids, IL: Zondervan Publishing House, 1970.

Schep, John A. *Baptism in the Holy Spirit*. Plainfield, NJ: Logos International, 1972.

Schlink, Basileau. *Ruled by the Spirit*. Minneapolis, MN: Dimension Books, 1969.

Schultz, D.Y. *The Paraclete*. New York, NY: Christian Alliance Publishers, 1903.

Scofield, Cyrus Ingerson. *Plain Papers on the Doctrine of the Holy Spirit*. Grand Rapids, MI: Baker House, 1889.

Scott, Ernest F. *I Believe in the Holy Spirit*. New York, NY: Abingdon Press, 1958.

Selby, Thomas G. *The Holy Spirit and Christian Privilege*. London: Charles H. Kelly, n.d.

Sherill, John L. *They Speak with Other Tongues*. Old Tappan, NJ: Fleming H. Revell Co., 1964.

Shoemaker, Samuel M. *With the Holy Spirit and with Fire*. New York, NY: Harper Brothers, 1960.

Simpson, Albert B. *Danger Lines in the Deeper Life*. New York, NY: Alliance Press Company, 1898.

——-*The Four-Fold Gospel*. Harrisburg, PA: Christian Publications, Inc., n.d.

——-*The Holy Spirit or Power from on High*. 1924, vol. 1.

——-*In Heavenly Places*. n.d.

——-*The Land of Promise*. Reprint 1969.

——-*The Spirit-Filled Church in Action*. 1975.

——-*Walking in the Spirit*. New York, NY: Alliance Press Co., 1886.

——-*When the Comforter Came*. New York, NY: Christian Alliance Publishing Company, 1911.

——*Wholly Sanctified*. Harrisburg, PA: Christian Publications Inc. 1925.

Smeaton, George. *The Doctrine of the Holy Spirit*. London: Banner of Truth, 1957.

Smith, Oswald J. *The Enduement of Power*. London: Marshall, Morgan and Scott, 1933.

——*The Spirit at Work*. 1939.

——*The Spirit Is Working*. 1939.

——*When He Is Come*. Toronto: Courier Office, 1929.

Stafford, E.A. *The Guiding Hand*. Toronto: W. Briggs, 1887.

Stagg, Frank. *The Holy Sirit Today*. Nashville, TN: Broadman Press. 1973.

Starkey, Lycurges Monroe. *The Work of the Holy Spirit*. New York, NY: Abingdon Press, 1962.

Stedman, Ray C. *Body Life*. Glendale, CA: Regal Books, 1972.

Stott, John R. *Baptism and Fullness*. Downers Grove, IL: InterVarsity Press, 1976.

Streeter, Burnett Hillman. *The Spirit*. London: MacMillan and Co., 1935.

Suenes, Henry Barclay. *The Holy Spirit in the Ancient Church*. Grand Rapids, MI: Baker Publishing House, 1966.

——*The Holy Spirit in the New Testament*. 1964.

Tari, Mel. *Like a Mighty Wind*. Carol Stream, IL: Creation House, 1972.

Taylor, John Vernon. *The Go-Between God*. Philadelphia, PA: Fort, 1973.

Thomas, William Henry Griffith. *The Holy Spirit of God*. Grand Rapids, MI: Eerdmans Publishing House, 1964.

————*The Christian Life and How to Live It*. Chicago, IL: Bible Institute Colportage Association, 1919.

Thompson, Fred P. *The Holy Spirit*. Ed. by Bruce L. Shelly. Wheaton, IL: Victor Books, 1978.

Torrey, Reuben Archer. *The Holy Spirit*. New York, NY: Fleming H. Revell Co., 1927.

————*The Person and Work of the Holy Spirit*. Grand Rapids, MI: Zondervan Publishing House.

Tozer, Aiden Wilson. *Gems from Tozer*. Bromley, Kent: Send the Light Trust, 1969.

————*How to Be Filled With the Holy Spirit*. Harrisburg, PA: Christian Publications, Inc., n.d.

————*Keys to the Deeper Life*. Grand Rapids, MI: Zondervan Publishing House, 1957.

————*Paths to Power*. Harrisburg, PA: Christian Publications Inc, n.d.

————*Ten Messages on the Holy Spirit*. 1968.

————*Tragedy in the Church: The Missing Gifts*. 1978.

————*When He is Come*. 1968.

Turner, Harry L. *The Voice of the Spirit*. Harrisburg, PA: Christian Publications Inc, 1951.

Tuttle, Robert G. *The Partakers*. Nashville, TN: Abingdon Press, 1974.

Underhill, Evelyn. *The Fruit of the Spirit*. London: Longman's Press, 1956.

————*The Life of the Spirit and the Life of Today*. London: Methuen and Company Limited, 1922.

Unger, Merrill F. *The Baptizing Work of the Holy Spirit*. Wheaton, IL: Van Kampen Press, 1953.

Van Dusen, Henry P. *Spirit, Son and Father*. New York, NY: Charles Scribner and Sons, 1958.

Walvoord, John F. *The Holy Spirit*. Wheaton, IL: Van Kampen Press, 1954.

------*The Holy Spirit at Work Today*. Lincoln, NE: Back to the Bible, 1973.

While, Reginald E. *The Answer Is the Spirit*. Philadelphia, PA: Westminster Press, 1979.

Williams, Charles. *The Descent of the Dove*. Grand Rapids. MI: Eerdmans Publishing House, 1939.

Williams, John. *The Holy Spirit, Lord and Life-Giver*. Neptune: Loizeau Bro., 1980.

Wilson, A.S. *Definite Experience*. London: M.M. & S., n.d.

Windish, Hans. *The Spirit-paraclete in the Fourth Gospel*. Trans. by James W. Cox Philadelphia, PA: Fortress Press, 1968.

Wirt, Sherwood E., *Afterglow*. Grand Rapids, MI: Zondervan Publishing House, 1976.

Wood, Arthur Skevington. *Life by the Spirit*. Grand Rapids, MI: Zondervan Publishing House, 1963.

Wood, Leon James, *The Holy Spirit in the Old Testament*. Grand Rapids, MI: Zondervan Publisning House, 1976.

Yates, John Edmund. *The Spirit and the Kingdom*. London: S.P.C.K., 1963.

Yohn, Rich. *Discover Your Spiritual Gift and Use It*. Wheaton, IL: Tyndale House Publishers, Inc., 1974.

Young, John Terry. *The Spirit Within You*. Nashville, TN: Broadman Press, 1977.